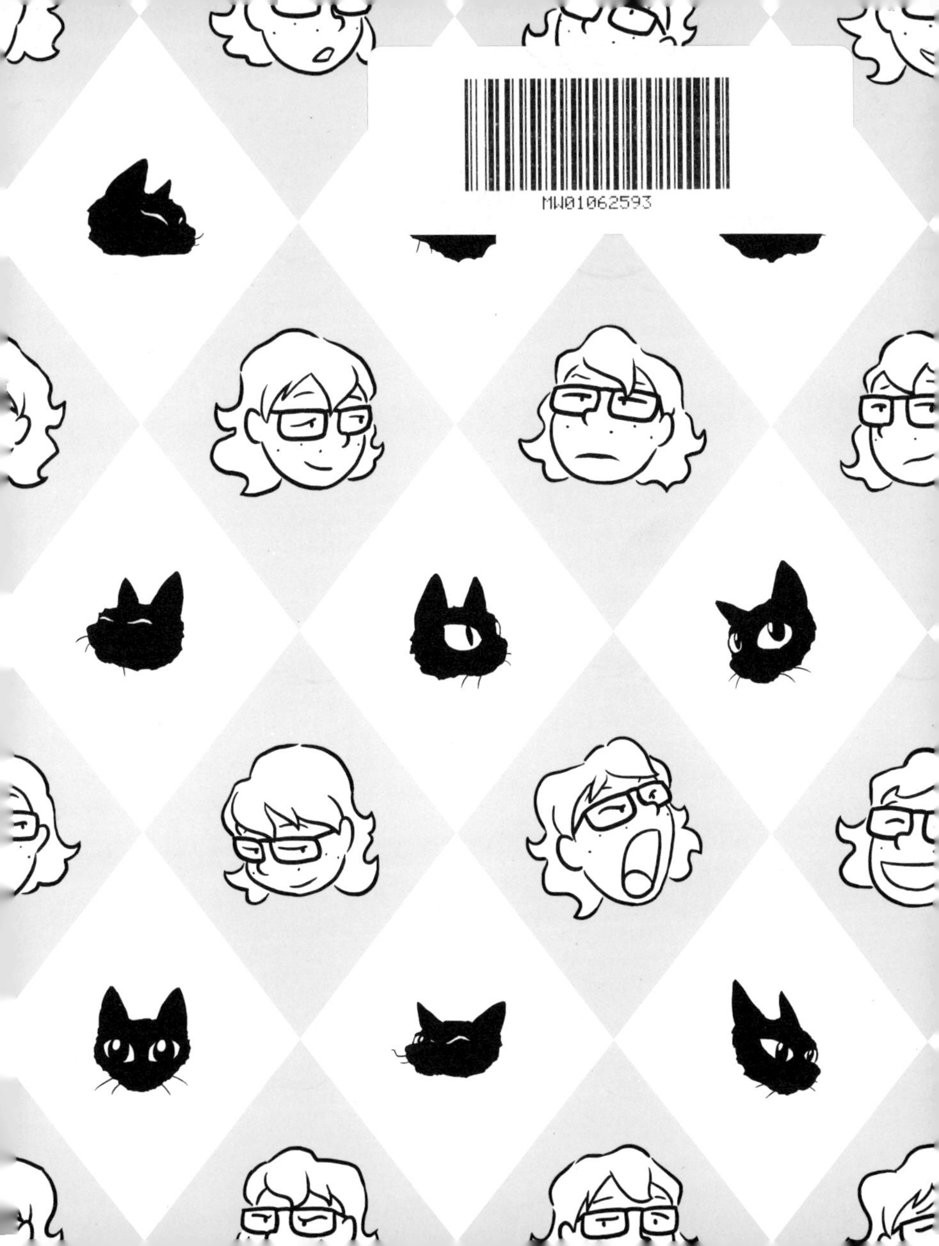

RASCAL

JEAN-LUC DEGLIN

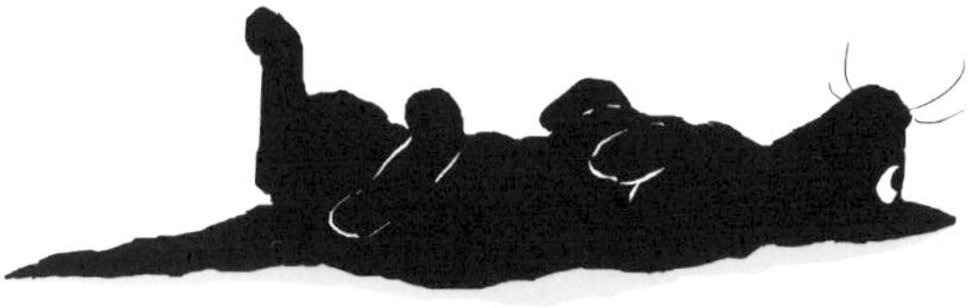

Top Shelf Productions

ISBN: 978-1-60309-463-4   23 22 21 20   1 2 3 4

Published by Top Shelf Productions, PO Box 1282, Marietta, GA 30061-1282, USA. Top Shelf Productions is an imprint of IDW Publishing, a division of Idea and Design Works, LLC. Offices: 2765 Truxtun Road, San Diego, CA 92106. Top Shelf Productions®, the Top Shelf logo, Idea and Design Works®, and the IDW logo are registered trademarks of Idea and Design Works, LLC. All Rights Reserved. With the exception of small excerpts of artwork used for review purposes, none of the contents of this publication may be reprinted without the permission of IDW Publishing. IDW Publishing does not read or accept unsolicited submissions of ideas, stories, or artwork. Printed in Korea.

Translated from the French by Edward Gauvin.

Editor-in-Chief: Chris Staros.
Edited by Leigh Walton.
Lettered by Tom B. Long.
Designed by Gilberto Lazcano.

Visit our online catalog at
www.topshelfcomix.com.

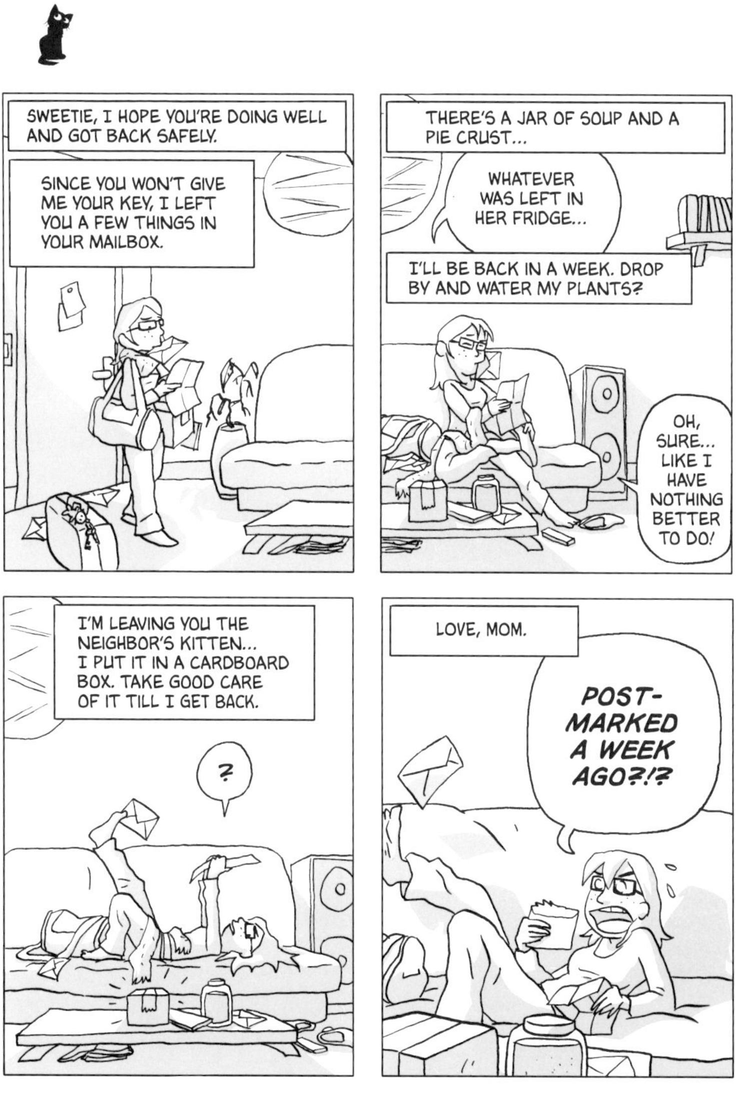
SWEETIE, I HOPE YOU'RE DOING WELL AND GOT BACK SAFELY.
SINCE YOU WON'T GIVE ME YOUR KEY, I LEFT YOU A FEW THINGS IN YOUR MAILBOX.
THERE'S A JAR OF SOUP AND A PIE CRUST...
WHATEVER WAS LEFT IN HER FRIDGE...
I'LL BE BACK IN A WEEK. DROP BY AND WATER MY PLANTS?
OH, SURE... LIKE I HAVE NOTHING BETTER TO DO!
I'M LEAVING YOU THE NEIGHBOR'S KITTEN... I PUT IT IN A CARDBOARD BOX. TAKE GOOD CARE OF IT TILL I GET BACK.
?
LOVE, MOM.
POST-MARKED A WEEK AGO?!?

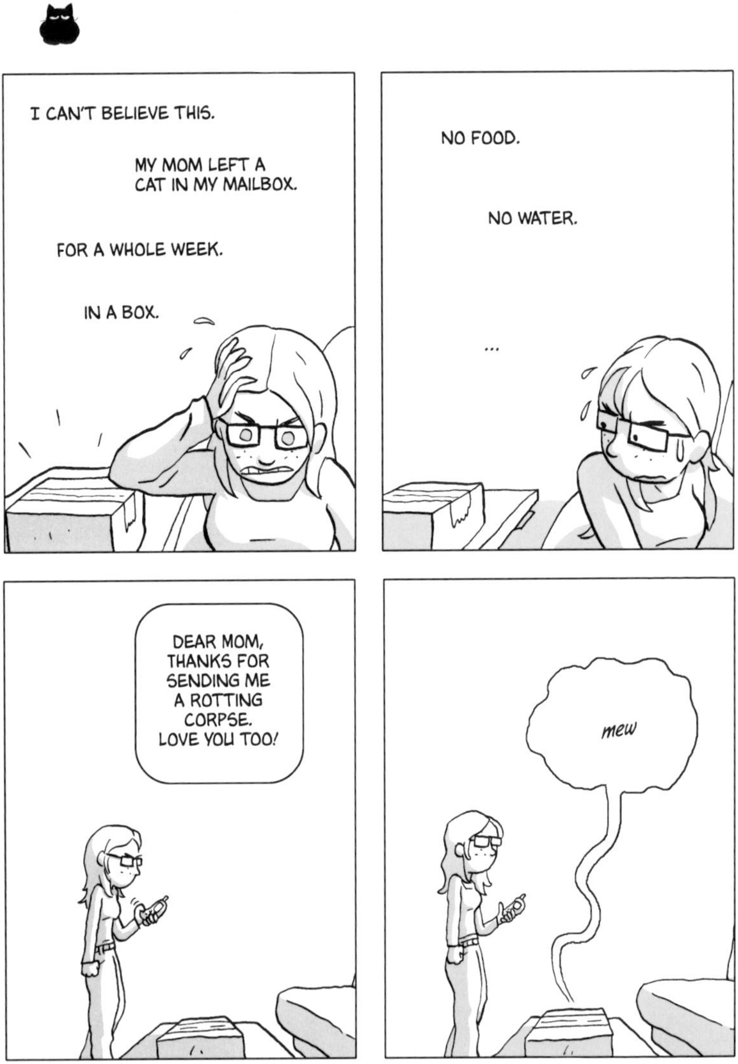
I CAN'T BELIEVE THIS.
MY MOM LEFT A CAT IN MY MAILBOX.
FOR A WHOLE WEEK.
IN A BOX.
NO FOOD.
NO WATER.
...
DEAR MOM, THANKS FOR SENDING ME A ROTTING CORPSE. LOVE YOU TOO!
mew

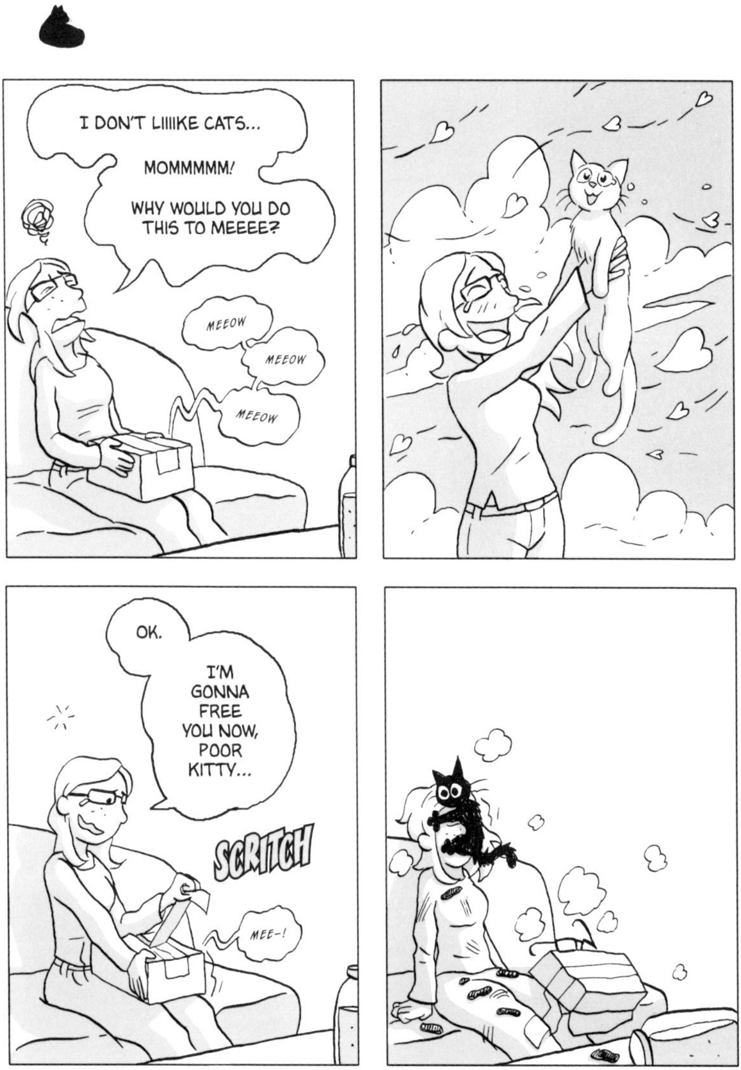
I DON'T LIIIIKE CATS...
MOMMMMM!
WHY WOULD YOU DO THIS TO MEEEE?
MEEOW
MEEOW
MEEOW
OK.
I'M GONNA FREE YOU NOW, POOR KITTY...
SCRITCH
MEE-!

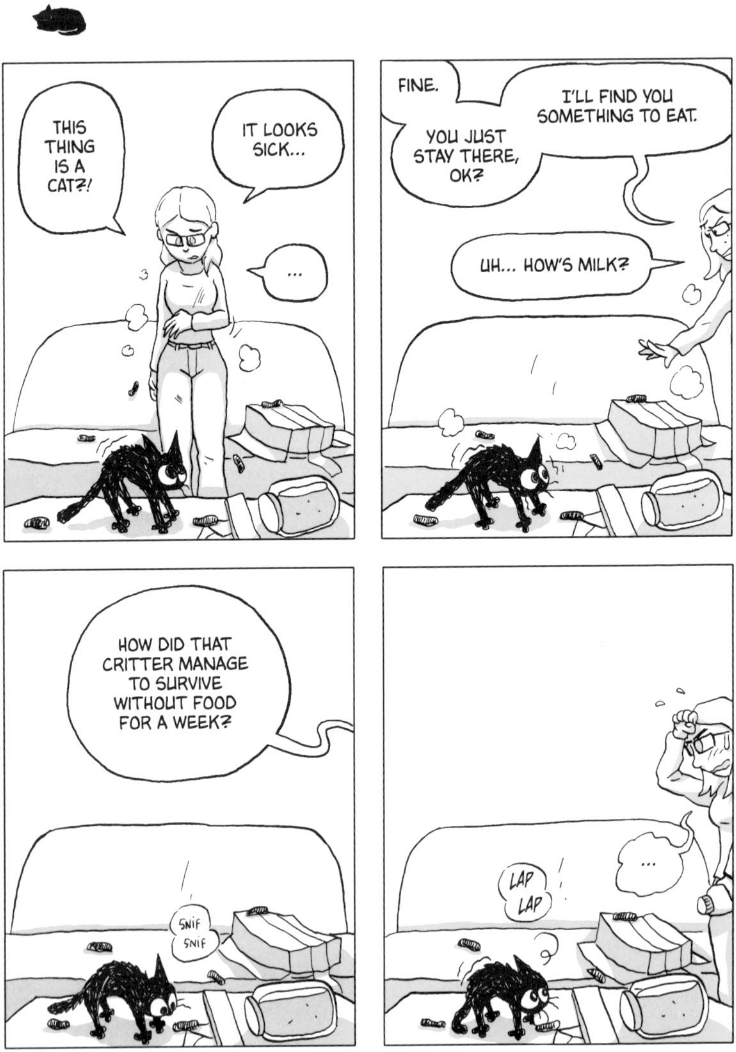
THIS THING IS A CAT?!
IT LOOKS SICK...
...
FINE.
I'LL FIND YOU SOMETHING TO EAT.
YOU JUST STAY THERE, OK?
UH... HOW'S MILK?
HOW DID THAT CRITTER MANAGE TO SURVIVE WITHOUT FOOD FOR A WEEK?
SNIF SNIF
LAP LAP
...

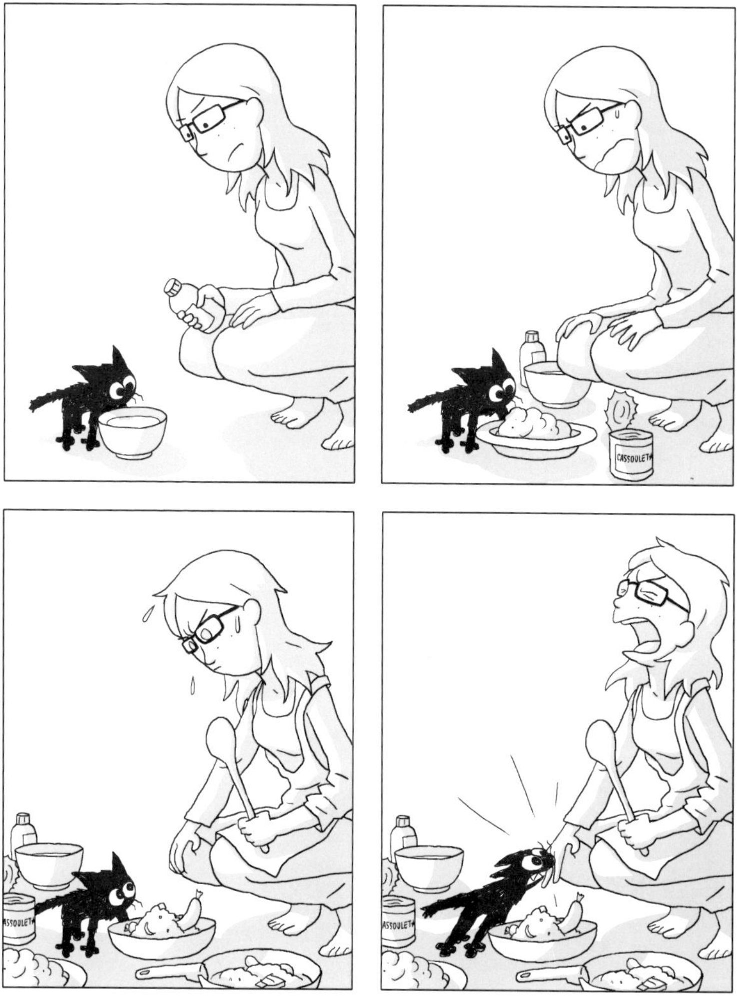
CASSOULET

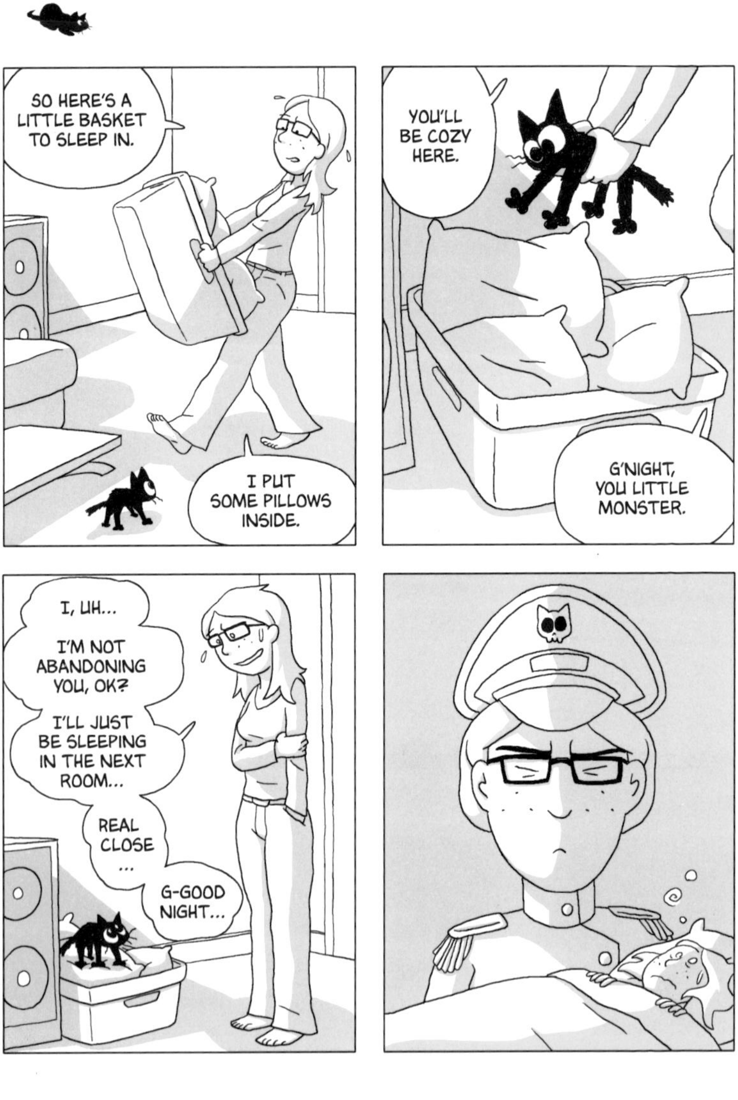
SO HERE'S A LITTLE BASKET TO SLEEP IN.
I PUT SOME PILLOWS INSIDE.
YOU'LL BE COZY HERE.
G'NIGHT, YOU LITTLE MONSTER.
I, UH...
I'M NOT ABANDONING YOU, OK?
I'LL JUST BE SLEEPING IN THE NEXT ROOM...
REAL CLOSE
...
G-GOOD NIGHT...

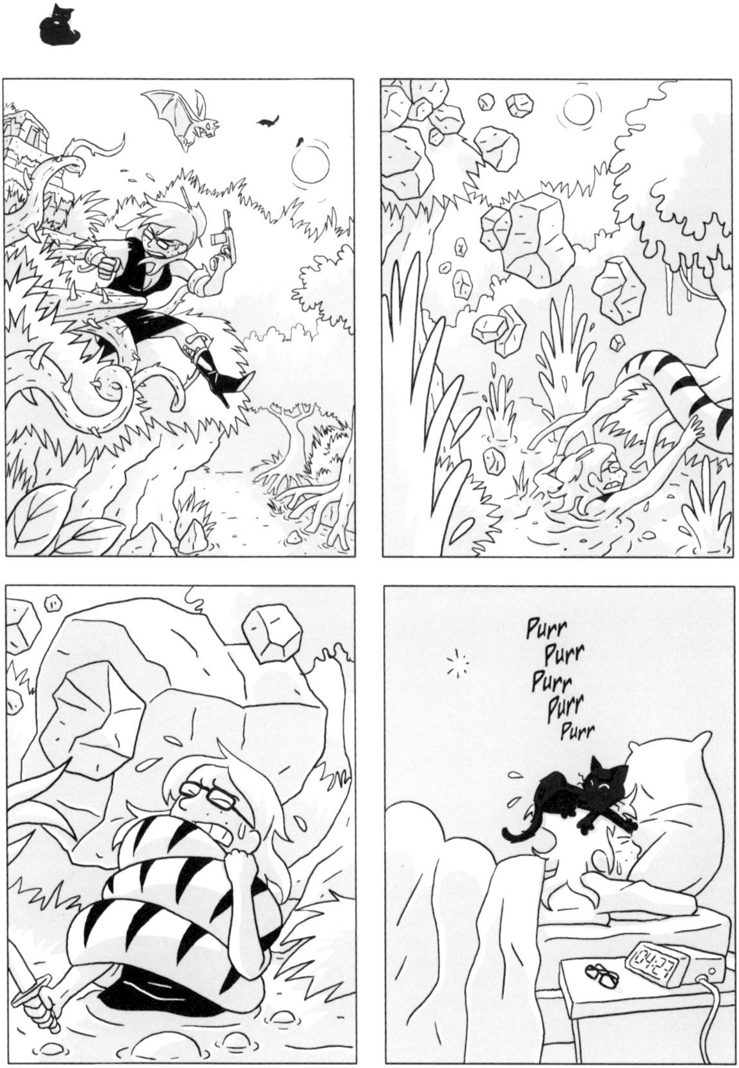
Purr
Purr
Purr
Purr
Purr
04:23

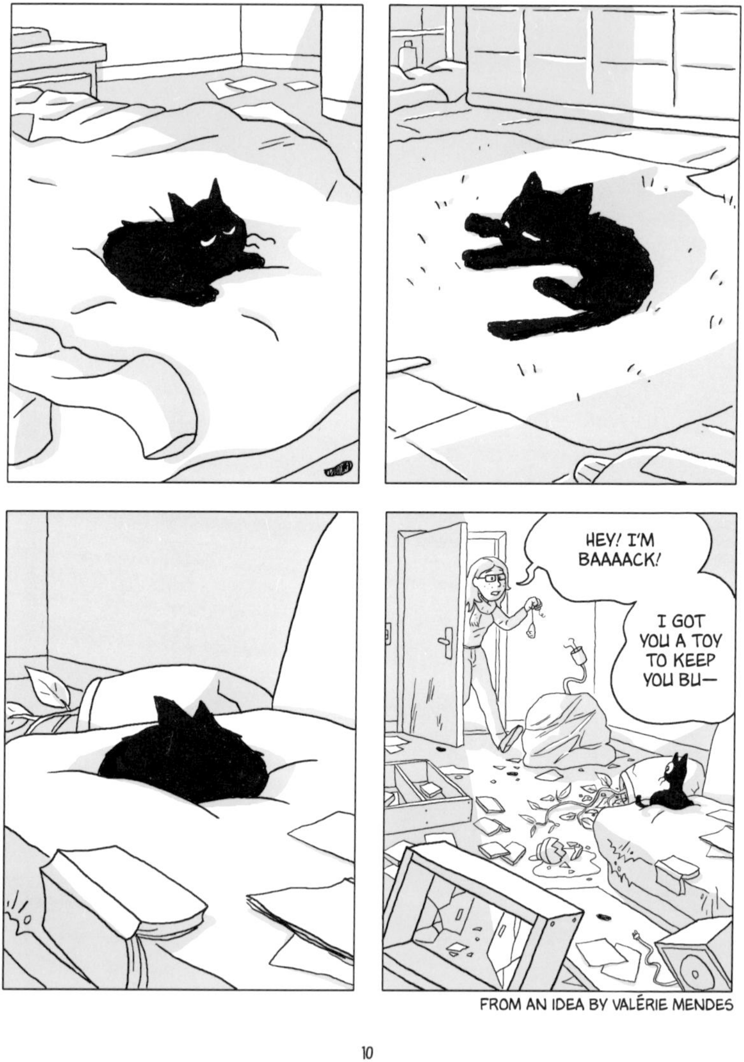
HEY! I'M BAAAACK!
I GOT YOU A TOY TO KEEP YOU BU—

FROM AN IDEA BY VALÉRIE MENDES

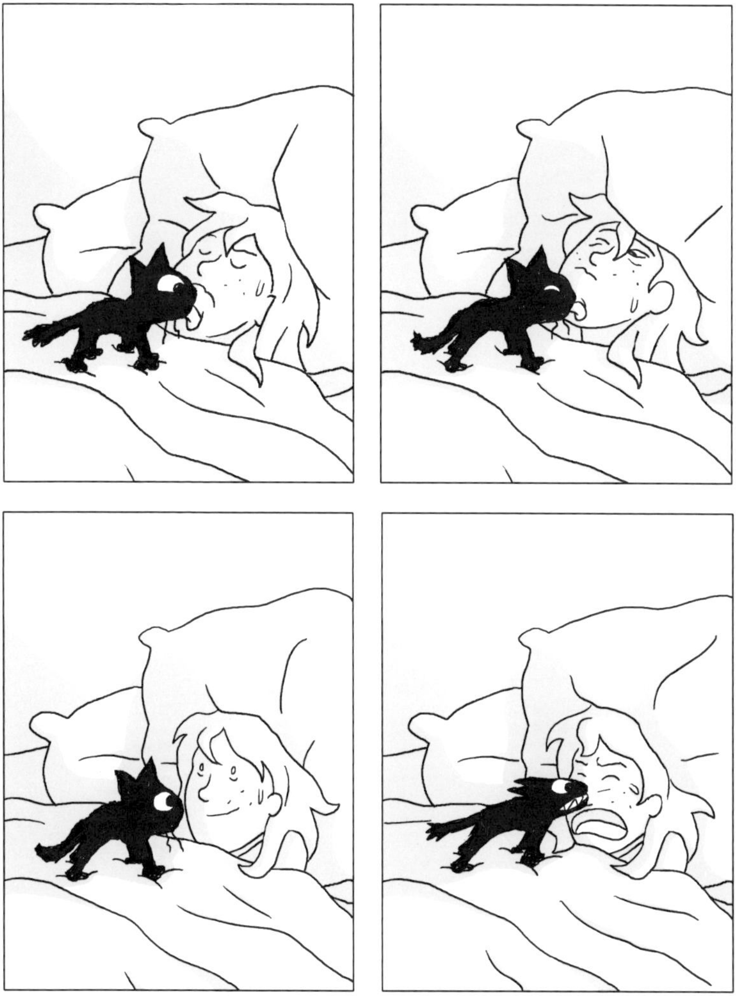

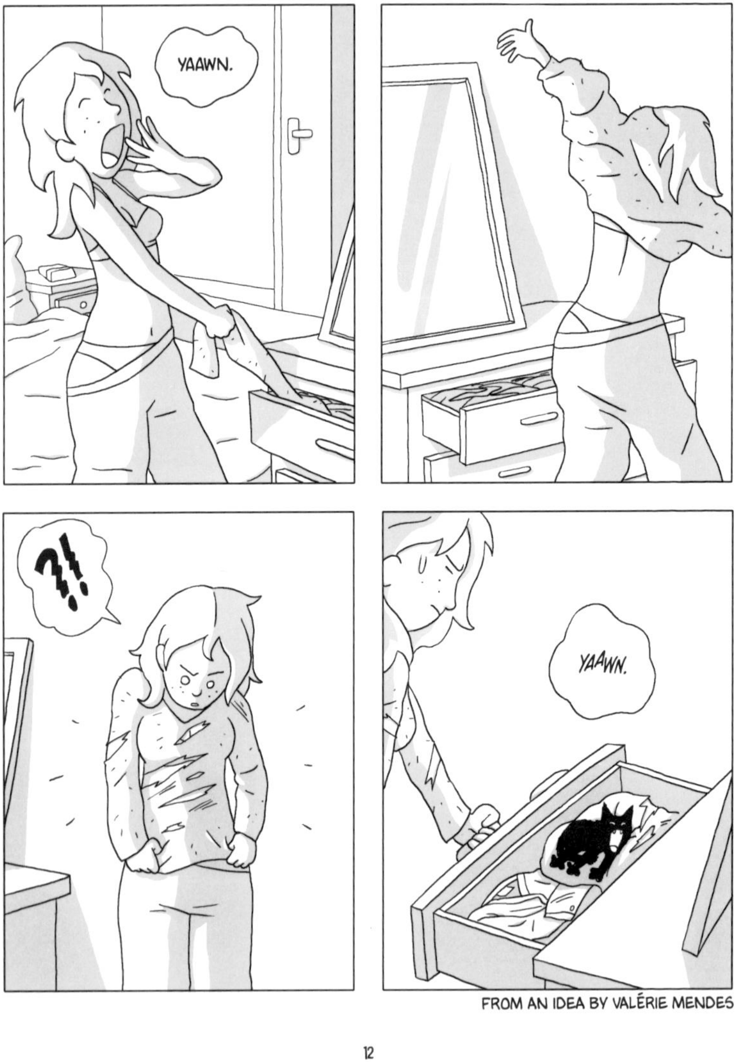
YAAWN.
?!
YAAWN.

FROM AN IDEA BY VALÉRIE MENDES

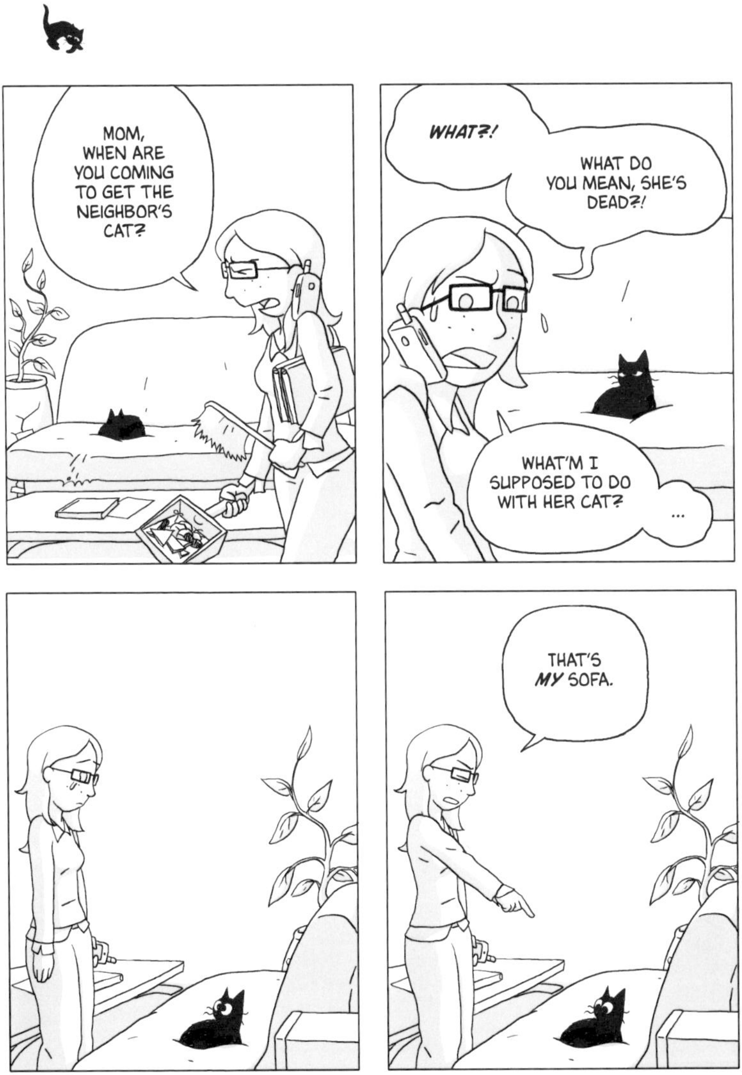
MOM, WHEN ARE YOU COMING TO GET THE NEIGHBOR'S CAT?
WHAT?!
WHAT DO YOU MEAN, SHE'S DEAD?!
WHAT'M I SUPPOSED TO DO WITH HER CAT?
...
THAT'S *MY* SOFA.

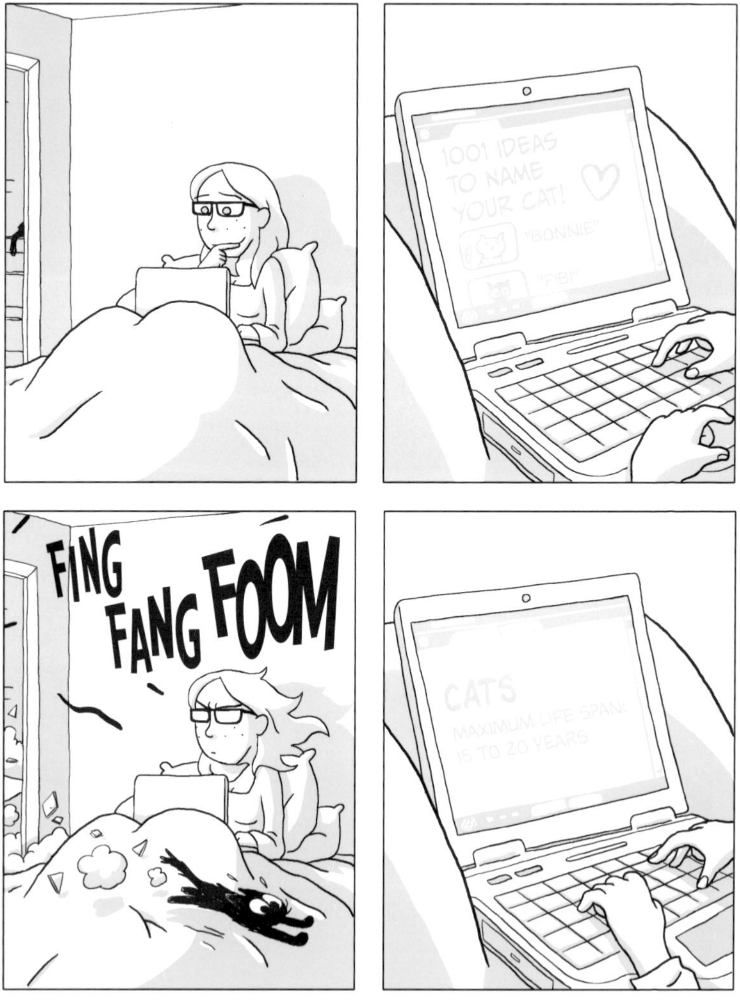
1001 IDEAS TO NAME YOUR CAT!
"BONNIE"
"FIBI"
FING FANG FOOM
CATS
MAXIMUM LIFE SPAN: 15 TO 20 YEARS

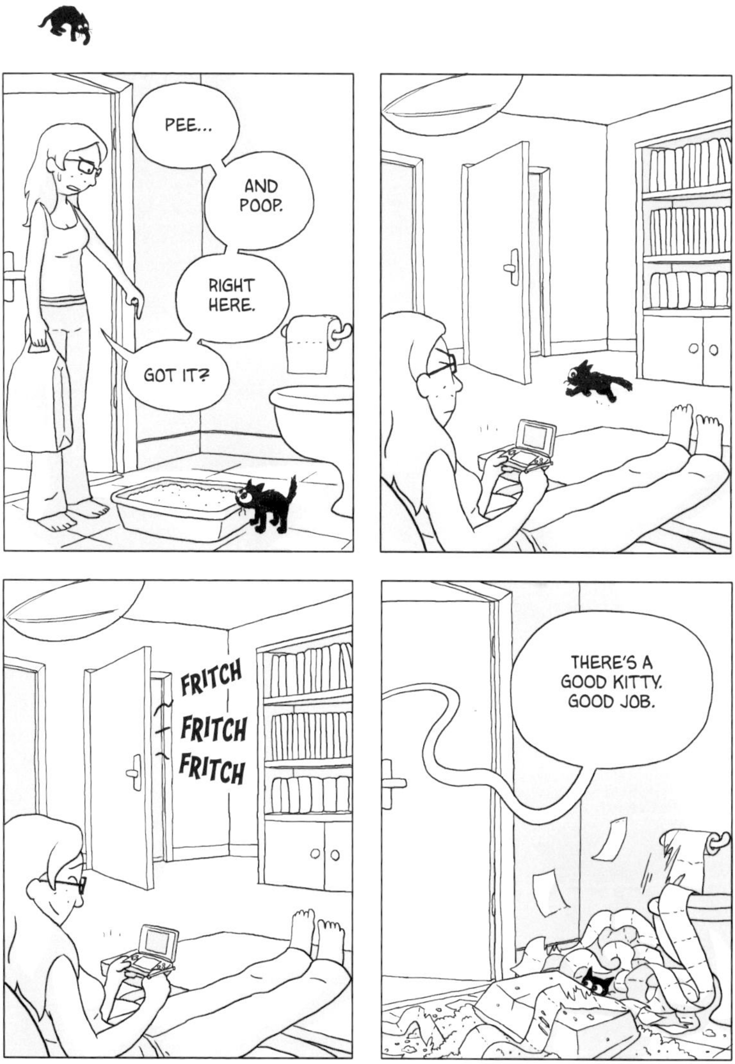
PEE...
AND POOP.
RIGHT HERE.
GOT IT?
FRITCH
FRITCH
FRITCH
THERE'S A GOOD KITTY. GOOD JOB.

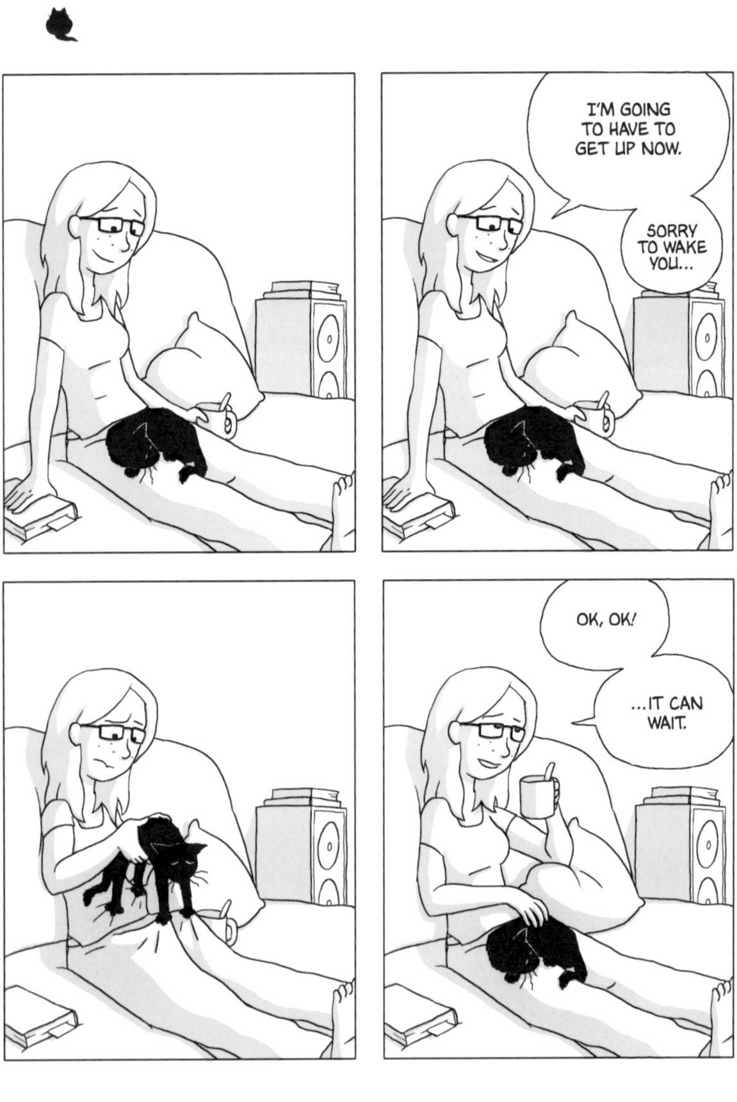
I'M GOING TO HAVE TO GET UP NOW.
SORRY TO WAKE YOU...
OK, OK!
...IT CAN WAIT.

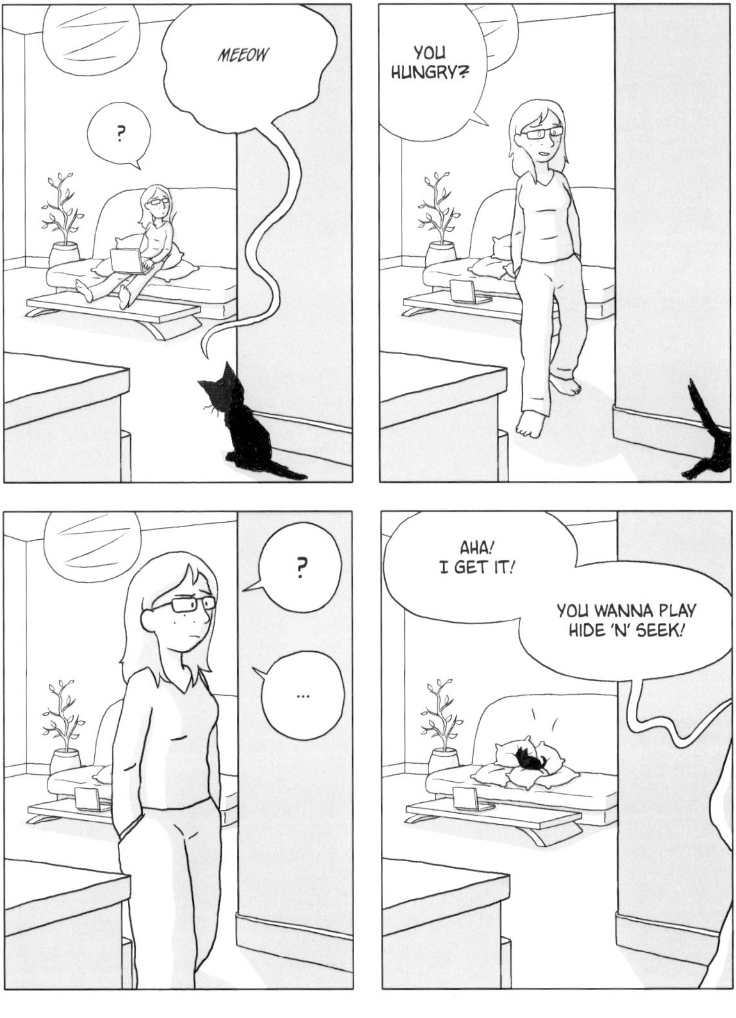
?
MEEOW
YOU HUNGRY?
?
...
AHA! I GET IT!
YOU WANNA PLAY HIDE 'N' SEEK!

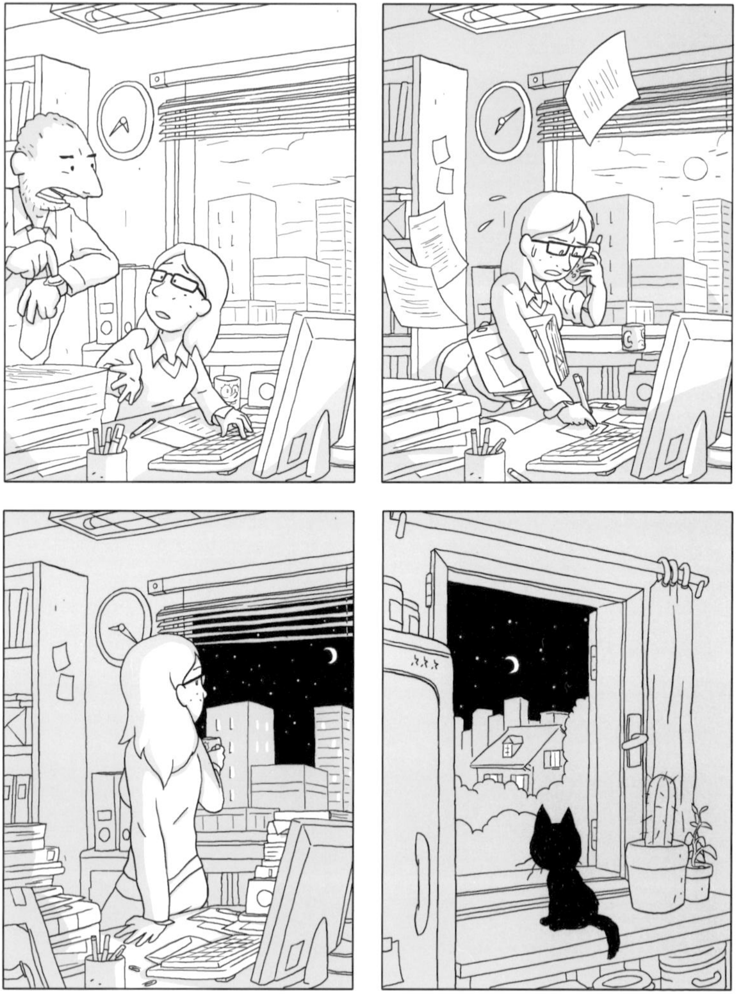

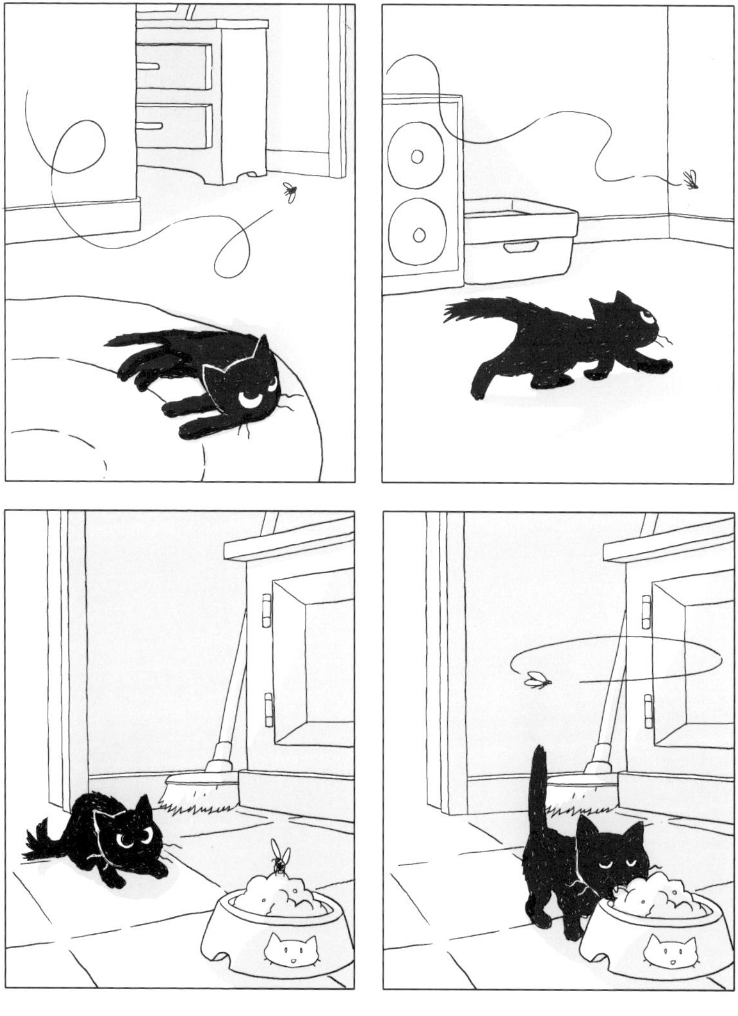

GROSS EAR...

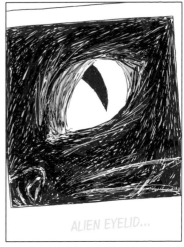

ALIEN EYELID...

MUTANT "THUMB"

I'VE GOT PROOF YOU'RE SOME KIND OF MONSTER!

NO USE PLAYING CUTE NOW!

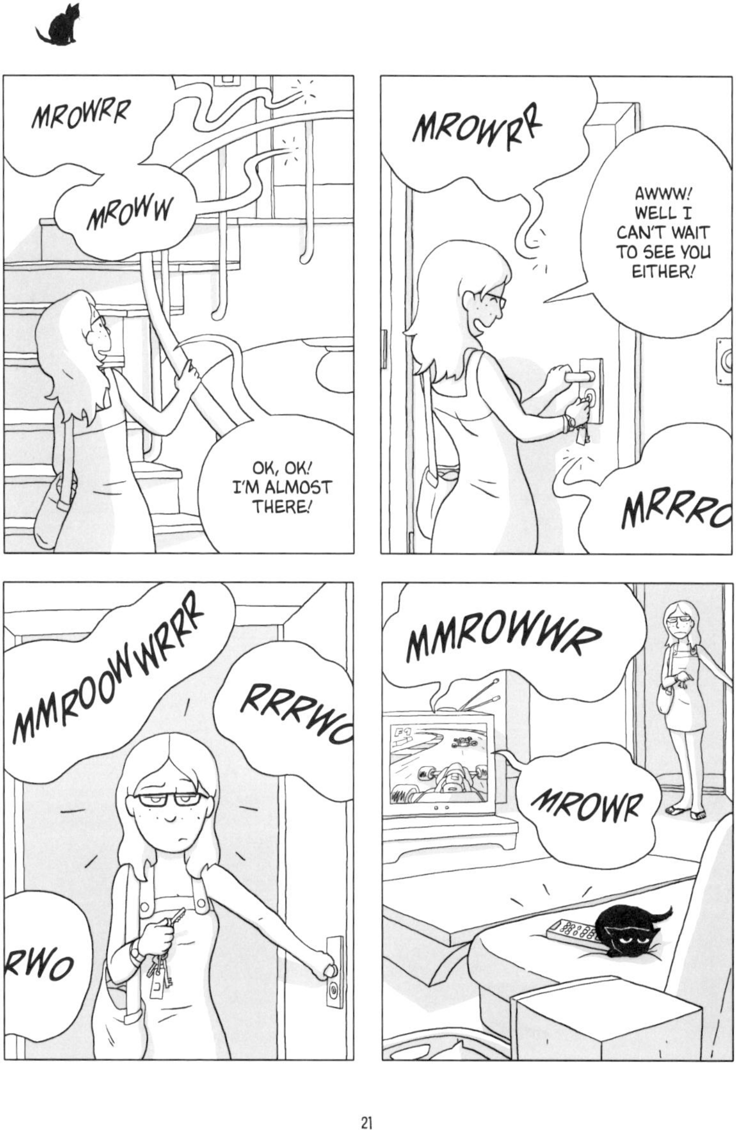
MROWRR
MROWW
OK, OK! I'M ALMOST THERE!
MROWRR
AWWW! WELL I CAN'T WAIT TO SEE YOU EITHER!
MRRRO
MMROOWWRRR
RRRWO
RWO
MMROWWR
MROWR

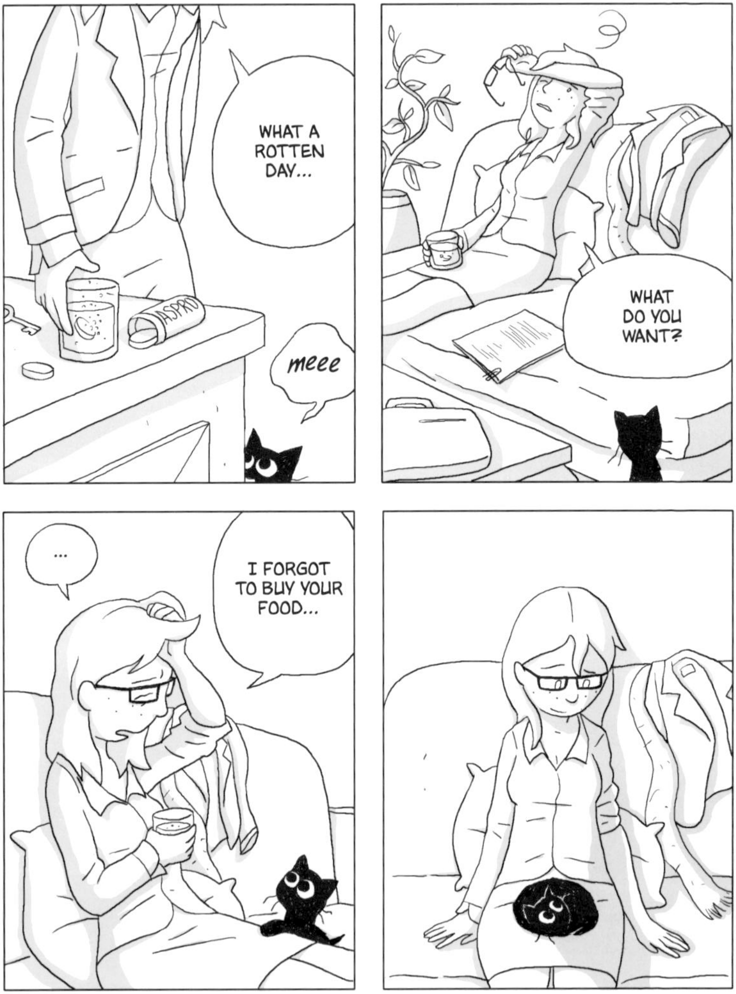
WHAT A ROTTEN DAY...
ASPRO
meee
WHAT DO YOU WANT?
...
I FORGOT TO BUY YOUR FOOD...

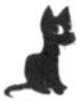

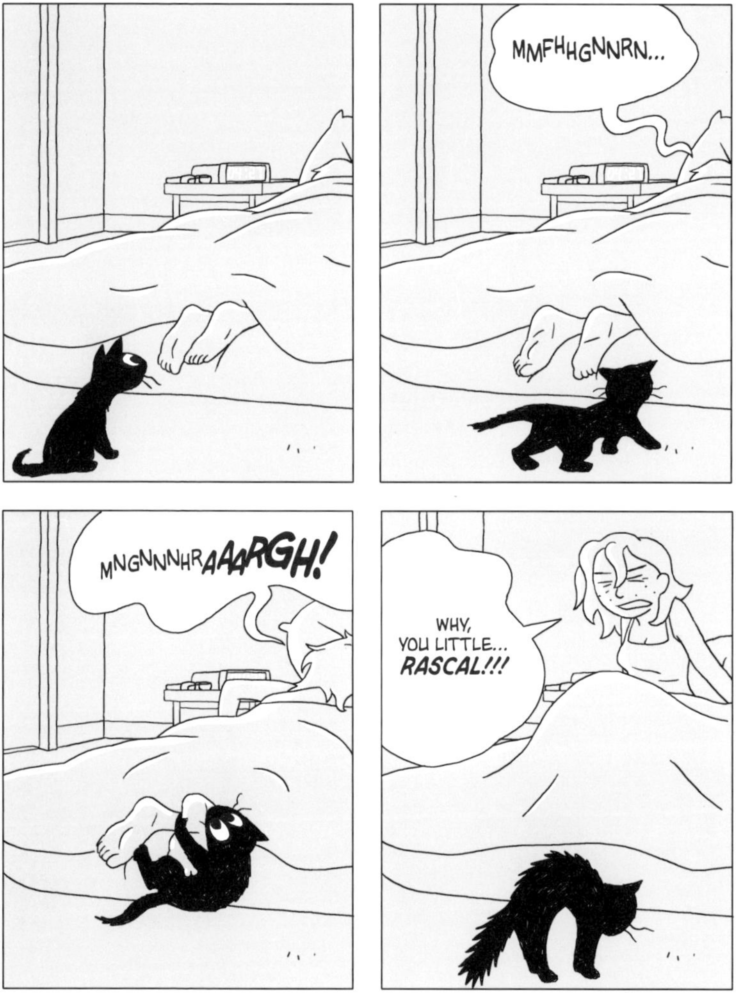
MMFHHGNNRN...
MNGNNNHRAAARGH!
WHY, YOU LITTLE... RASCAL!!!

FROM AN IDEA BY VALÉRIE MENDES

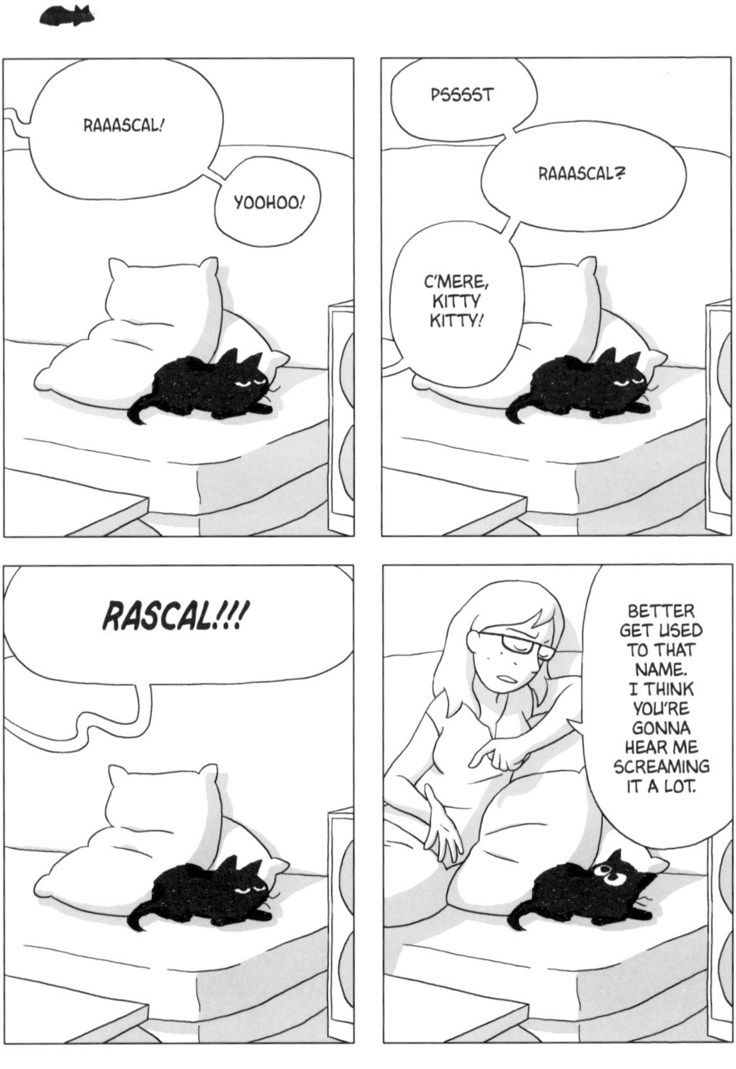
RAAASCAL!
YOOHOO!
PSSSST
RAAASCAL?
C'MERE, KITTY KITTY!
RASCAL!!!
BETTER GET USED TO THAT NAME. I THINK YOU'RE GONNA HEAR ME SCREAMING IT A LOT.

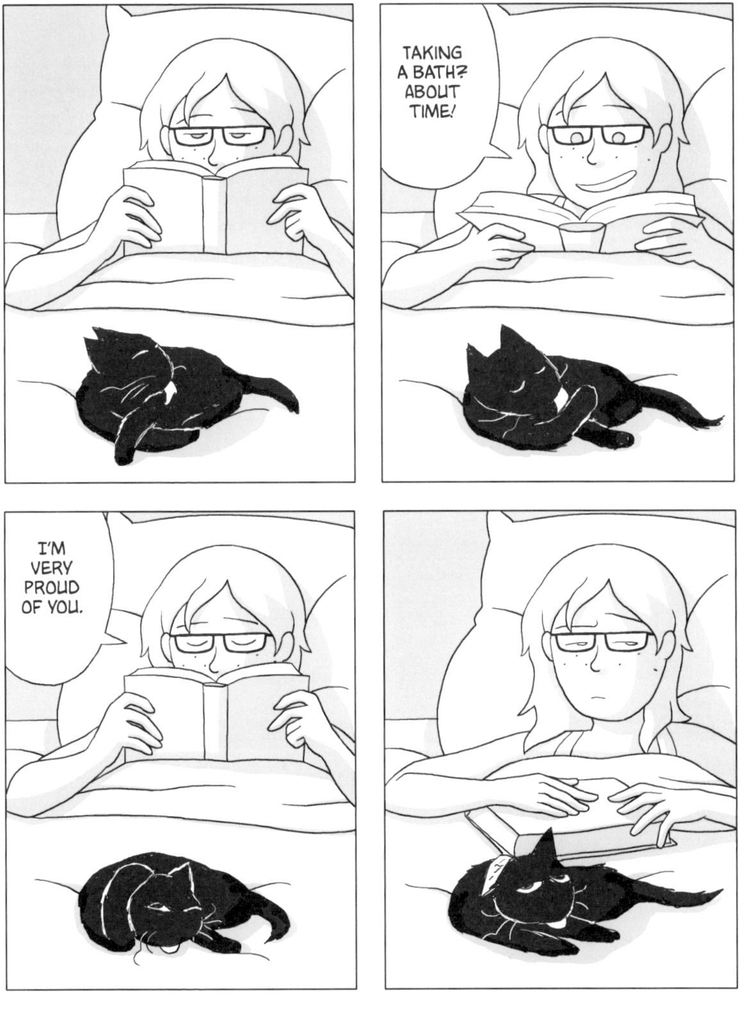
TAKING A BATH? ABOUT TIME!
I'M VERY PROUD OF YOU.

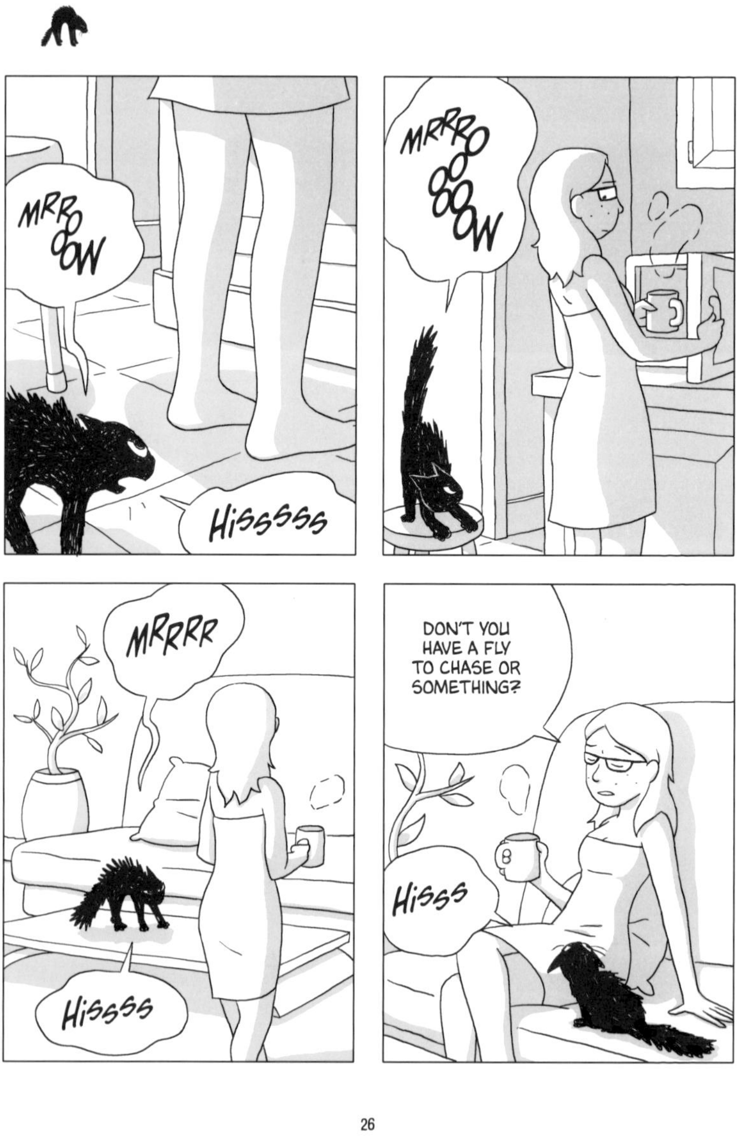
MRROOOW
HiSSSSS
MRRROOOOOOW
MRRRR
HiSSSS
DON'T YOU HAVE A FLY TO CHASE OR SOMETHING?
HiSSS

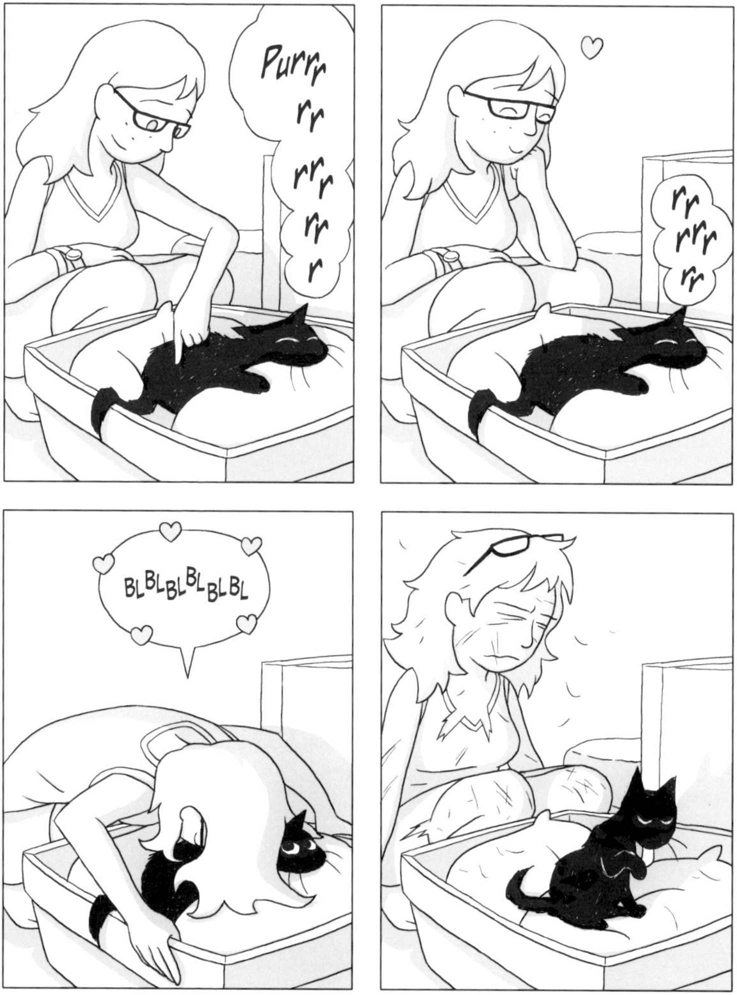
Purrr rr rrr rr r
rr rrr rr
BLBLBLBLBLBLBL

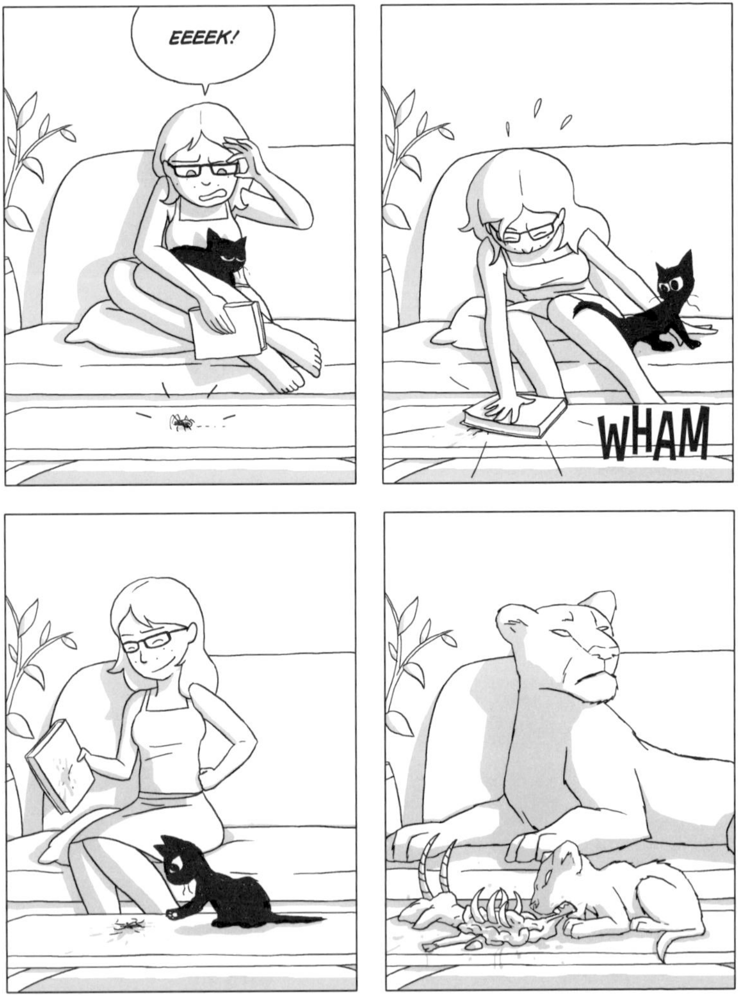
EEEEK!
WHAM

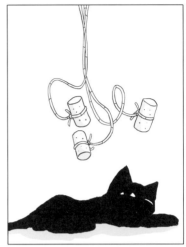

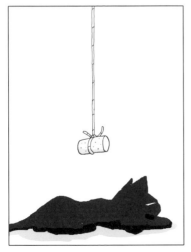

IF YOU KNOW ANY OTHER GAMES THAT DON'T INVOLVE ME BLEEDING, GIVE A SHOUT.

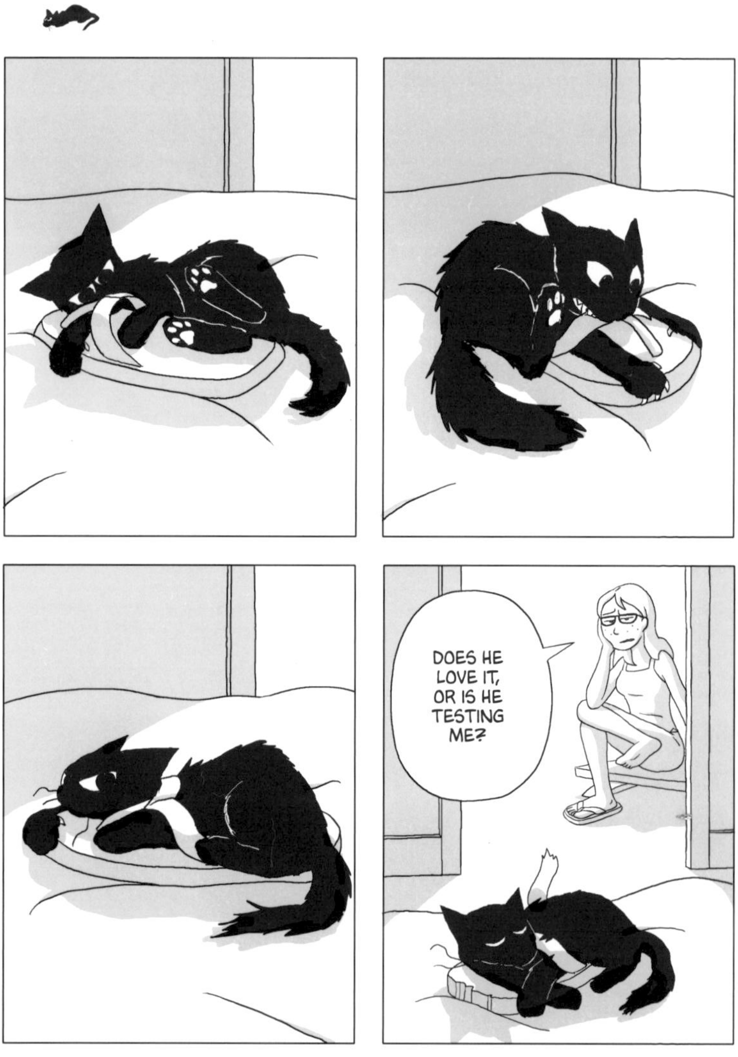
DOES HE LOVE IT, OR IS HE TESTING ME?

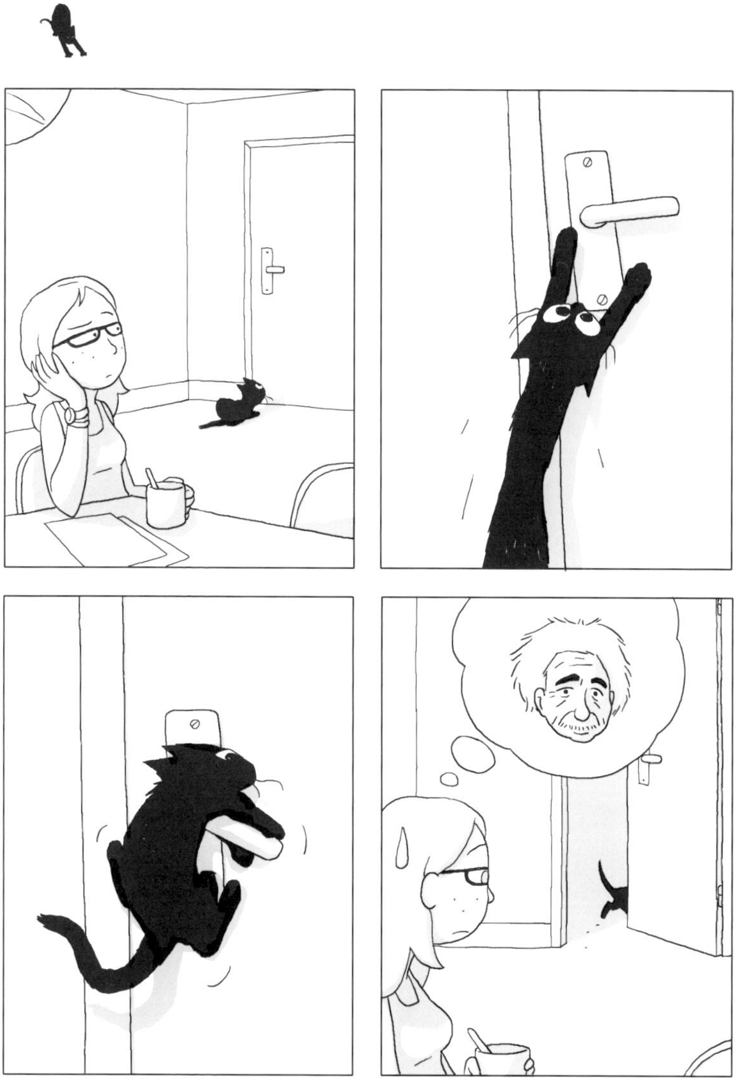

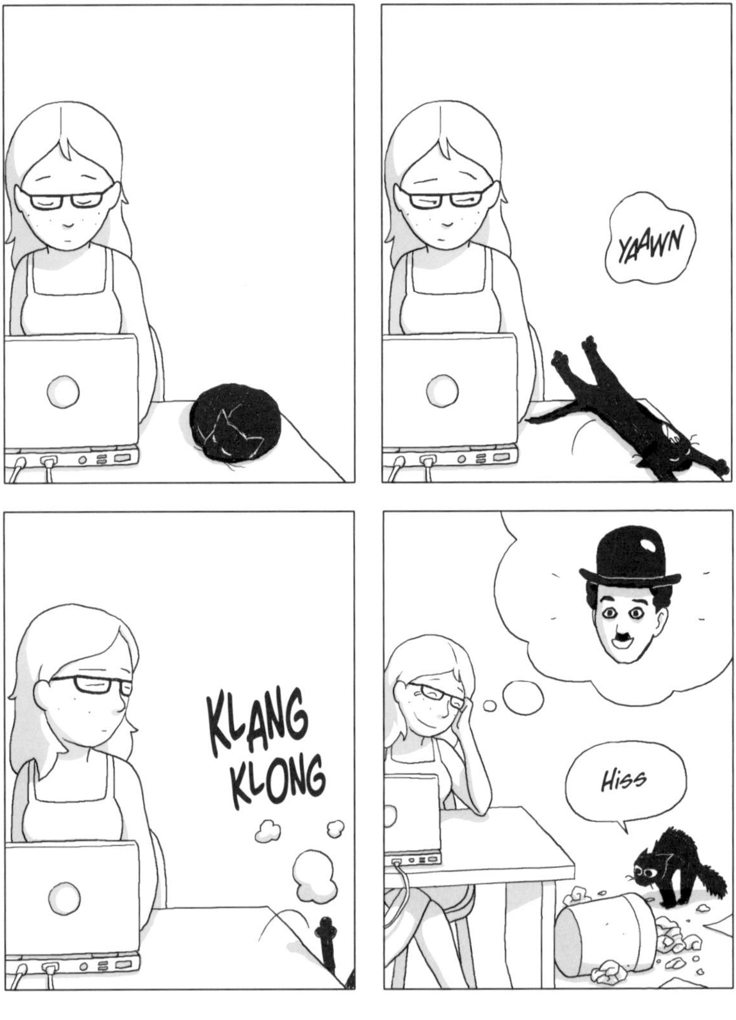
YAAWN
KLANG
KLONG
Hiss

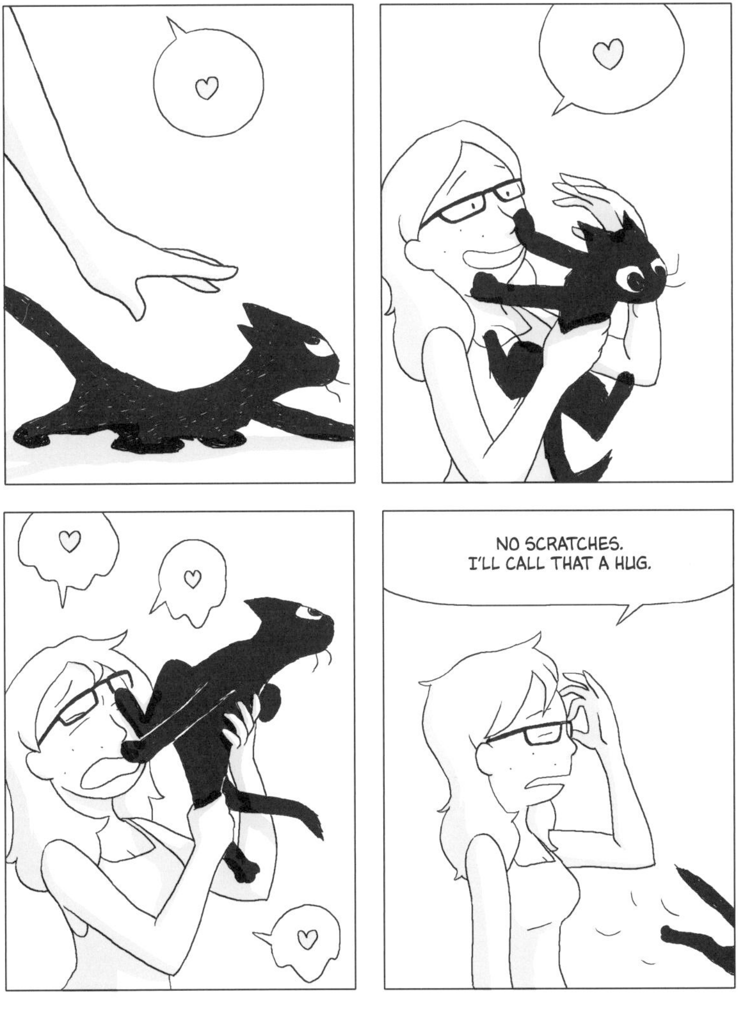
NO SCRATCHES.
I'LL CALL THAT A HUG.

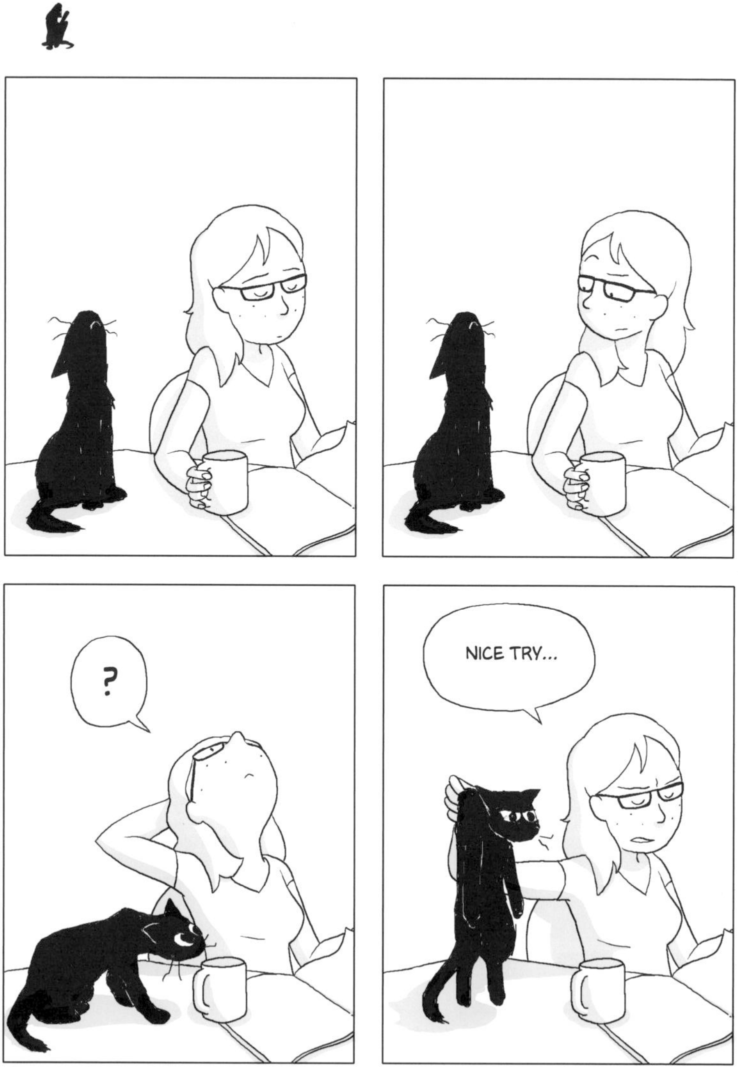
?
NICE TRY...

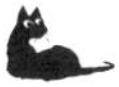

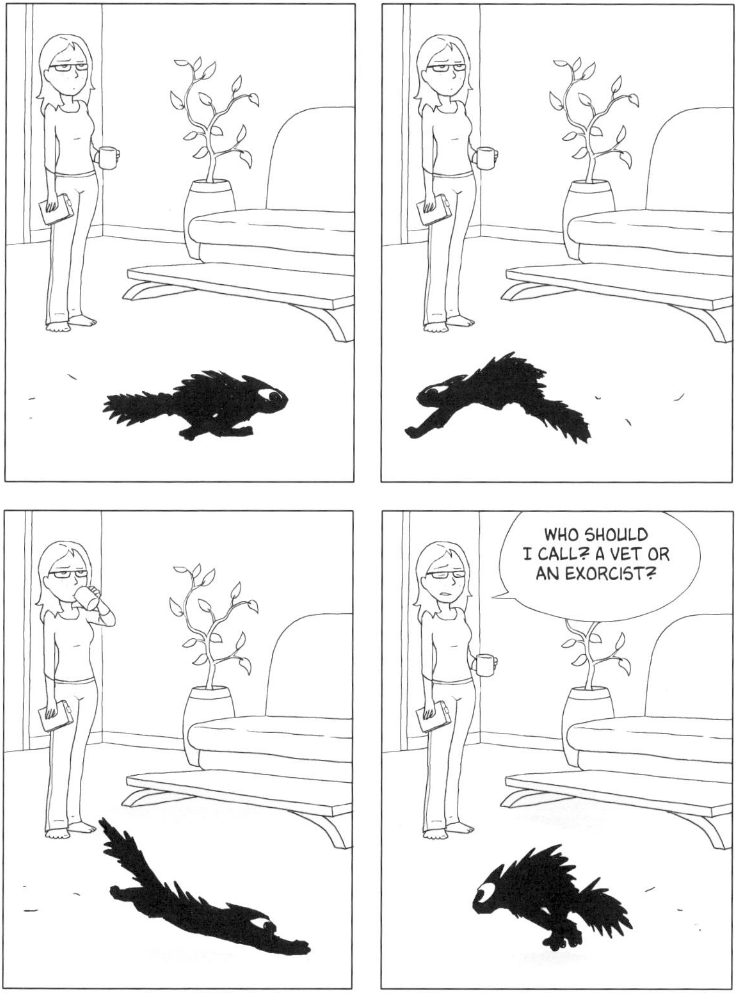
WHO SHOULD I CALL? A VET OR AN EXORCIST?

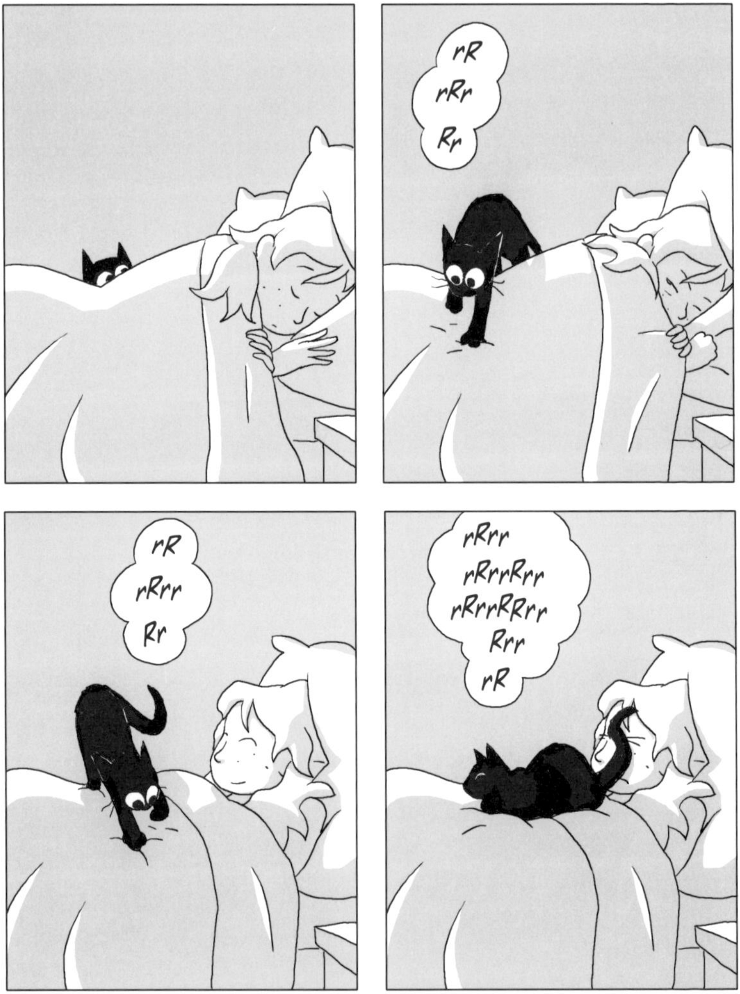
rR
rRr
Rr
rR
rRrr
Rr
rRrr
rRrrRrr
rRrrRRrr
Rrr
rR

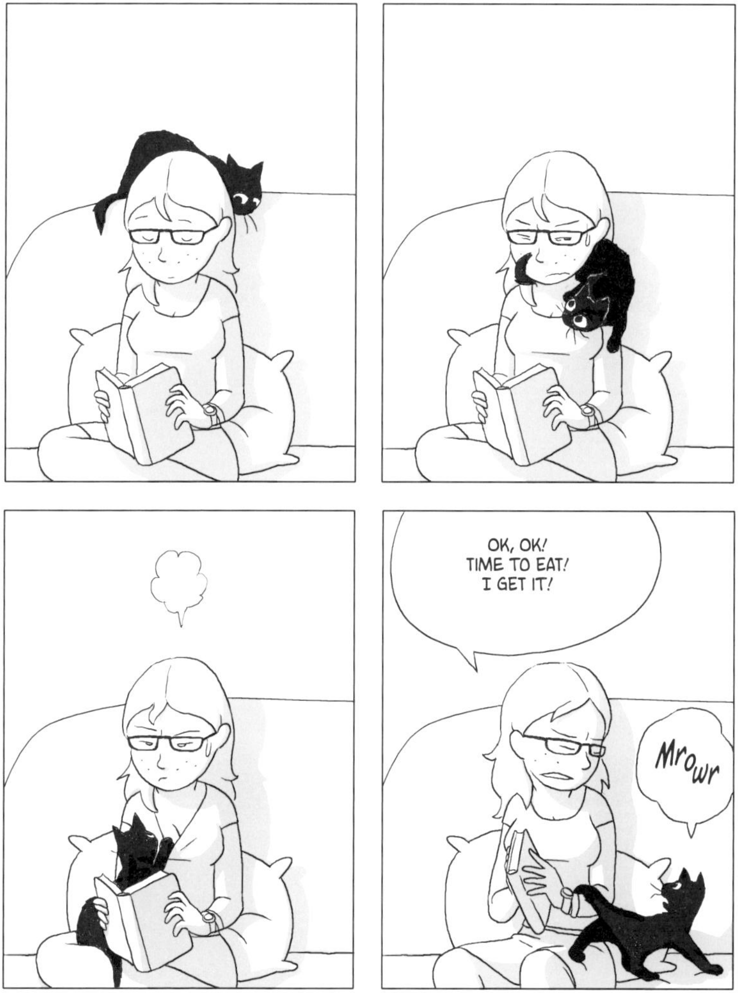
OK, OK!
TIME TO EAT!
I GET IT!
Mrowr

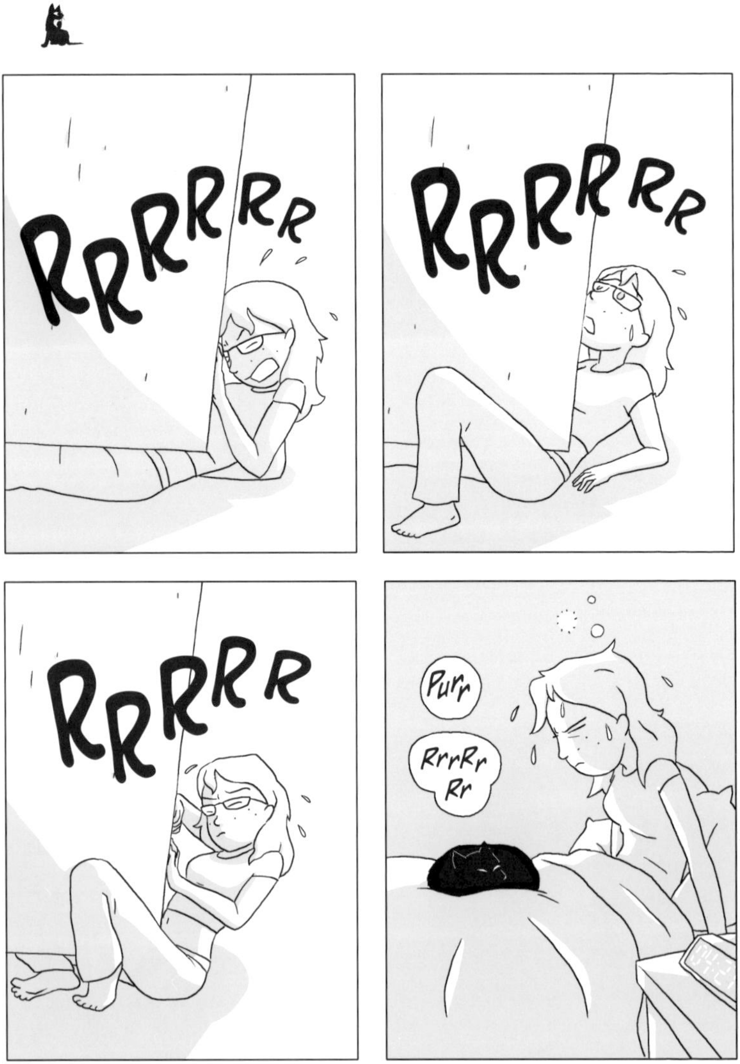
RRRRRR
RRRRRRR
RRRRR
Purr
RrrRr Rr

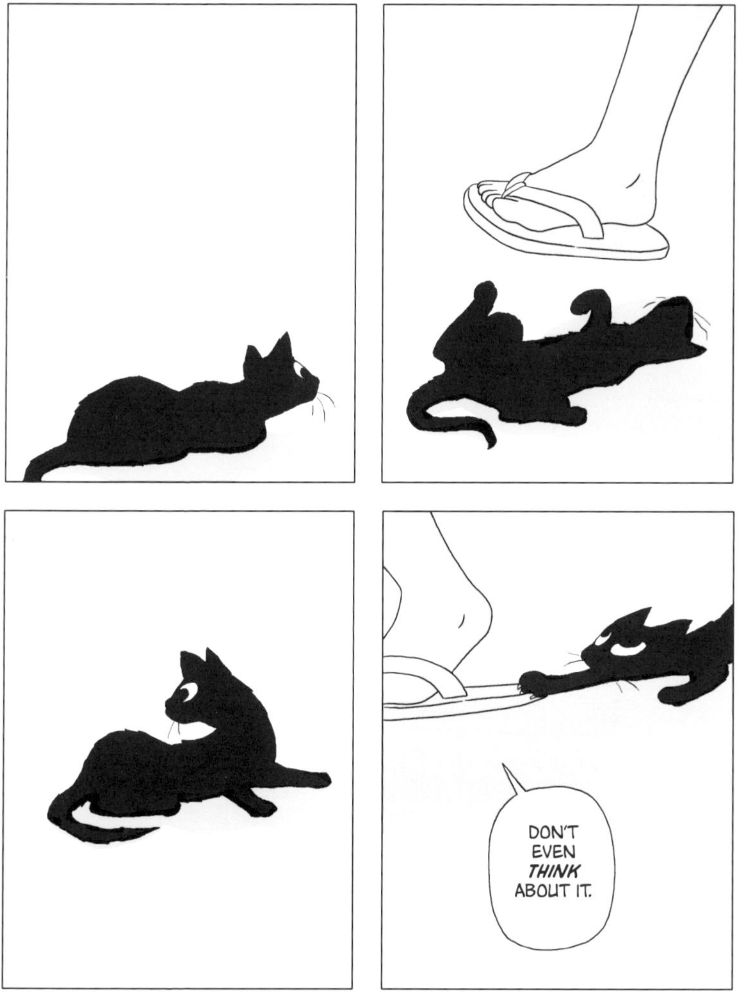
DON'T EVEN *THINK* ABOUT IT.

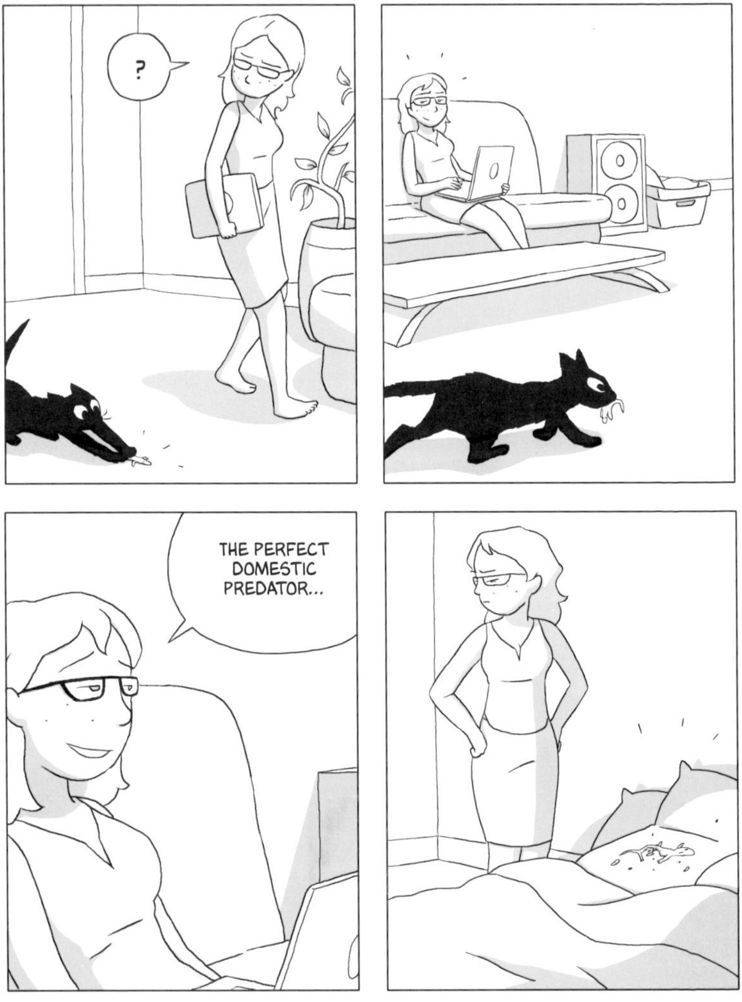
?
THE PERFECT DOMESTIC PREDATOR...

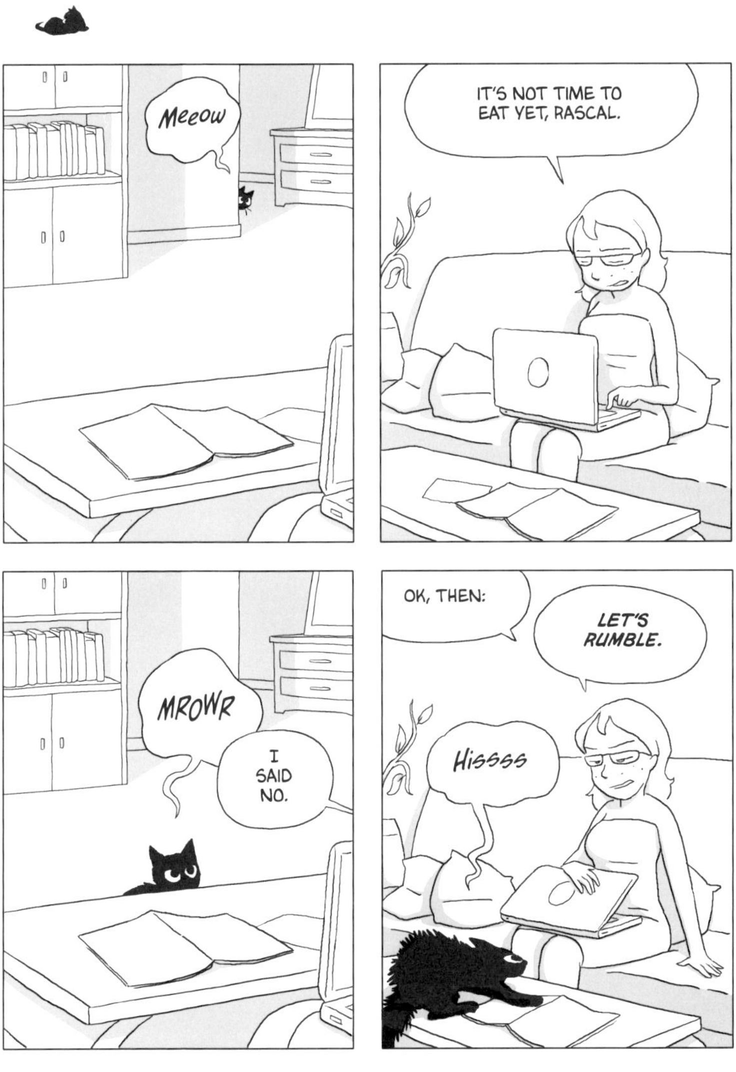
Meeow
IT'S NOT TIME TO EAT YET, RASCAL.
MROWR
I SAID NO.
OK, THEN:
LET'S RUMBLE.
Hissss

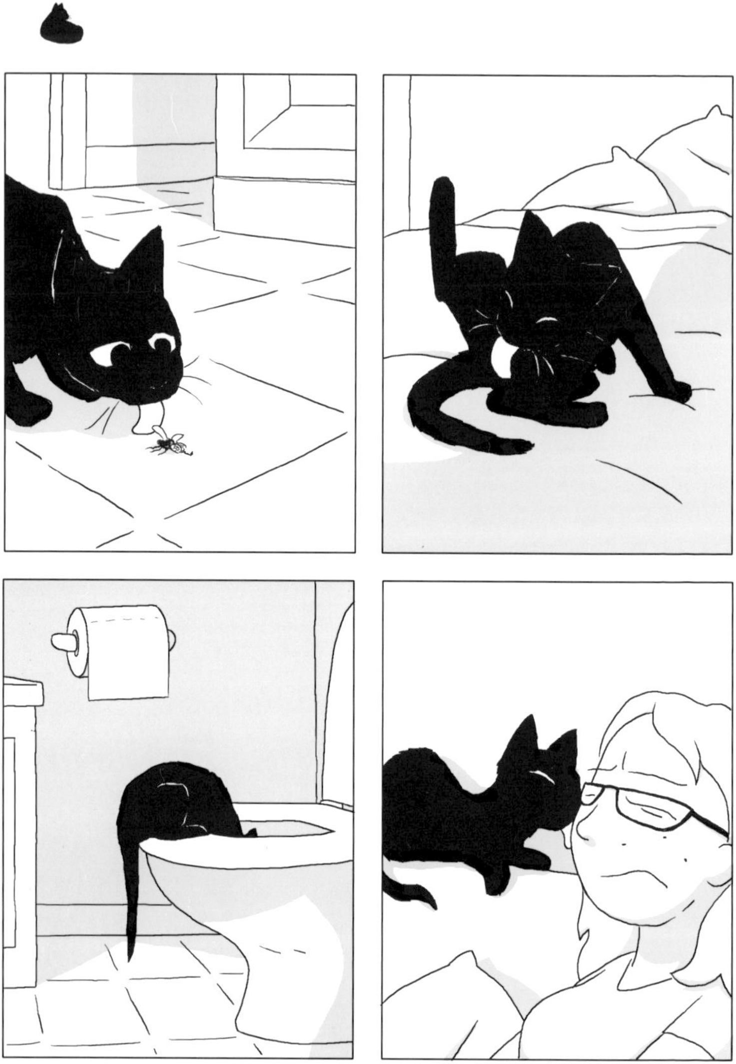

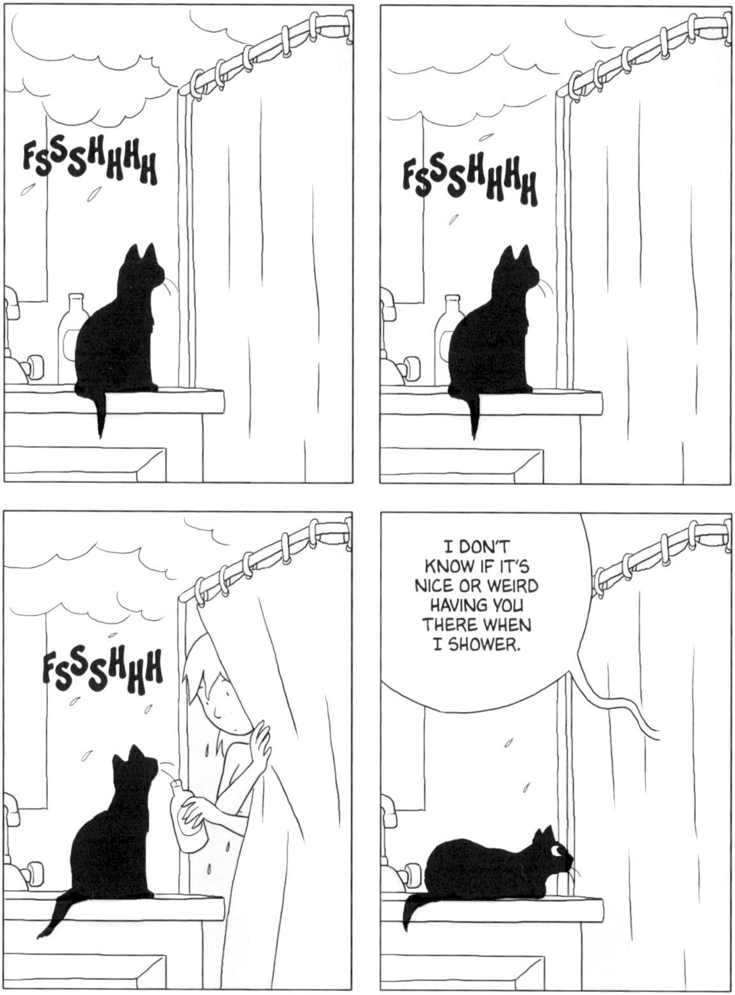
FSSSHHHH
FSSSHHHH
FSSSHHH
I DON'T KNOW IF IT'S NICE OR WEIRD HAVING YOU THERE WHEN I SHOWER.

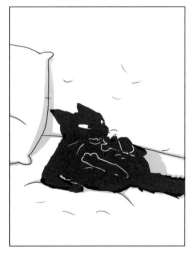

MY KINGDOM
FOR A NAIL FILE...

THIS IS *MY* SANDWICH.
STOP–
AAAARGH–
THIS IS INSANE!
YOUR BOWL IS LITERALLY *FULL* OF FOOD!

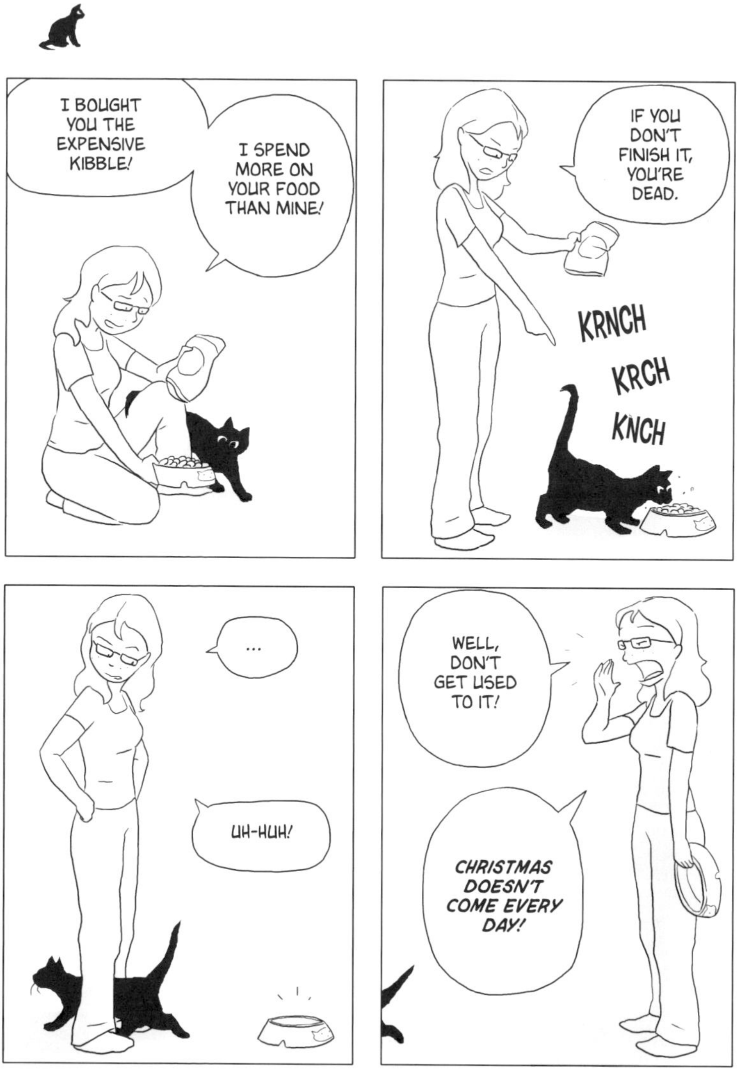
I BOUGHT YOU THE EXPENSIVE KIBBLE!
I SPEND MORE ON YOUR FOOD THAN MINE!
IF YOU DON'T FINISH IT, YOU'RE DEAD.
KRNCH
KRCH
KNCH
...
UH-HUH!
WELL, DON'T GET USED TO IT!
CHRISTMAS DOESN'T COME EVERY DAY!

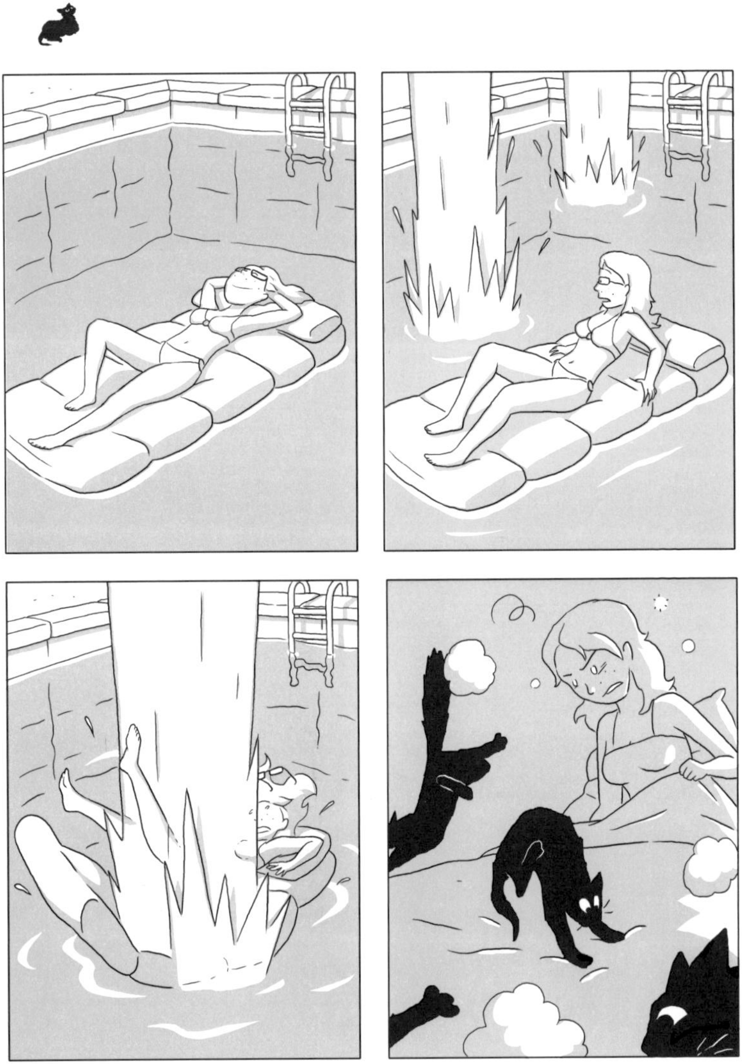

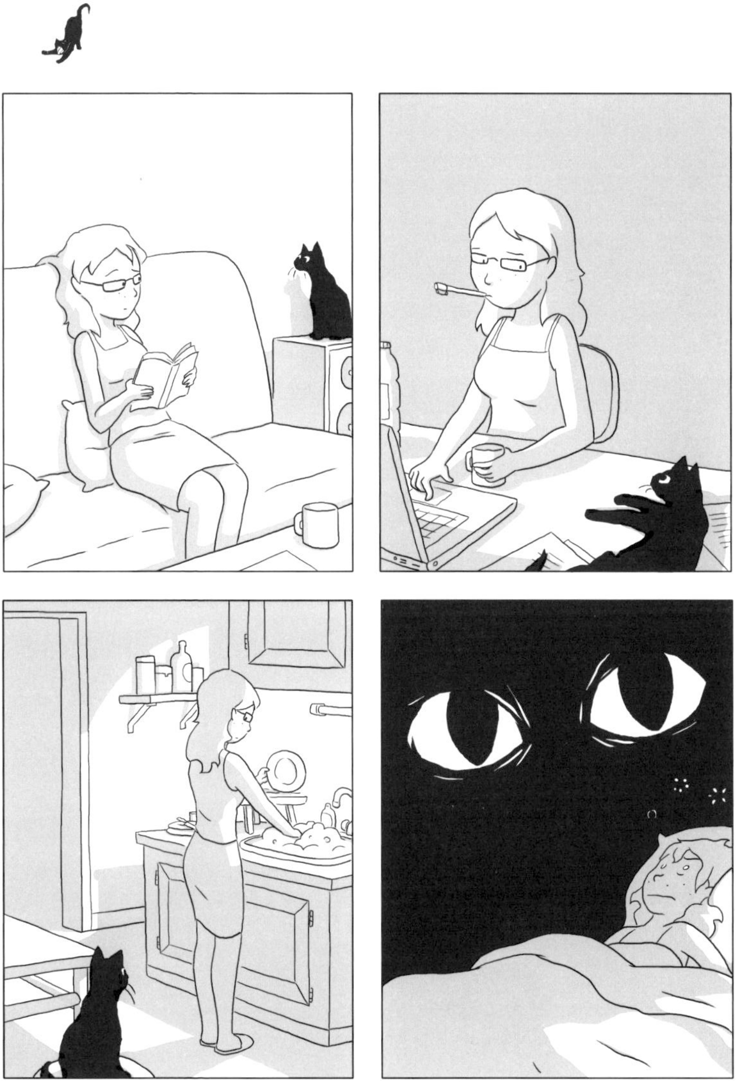

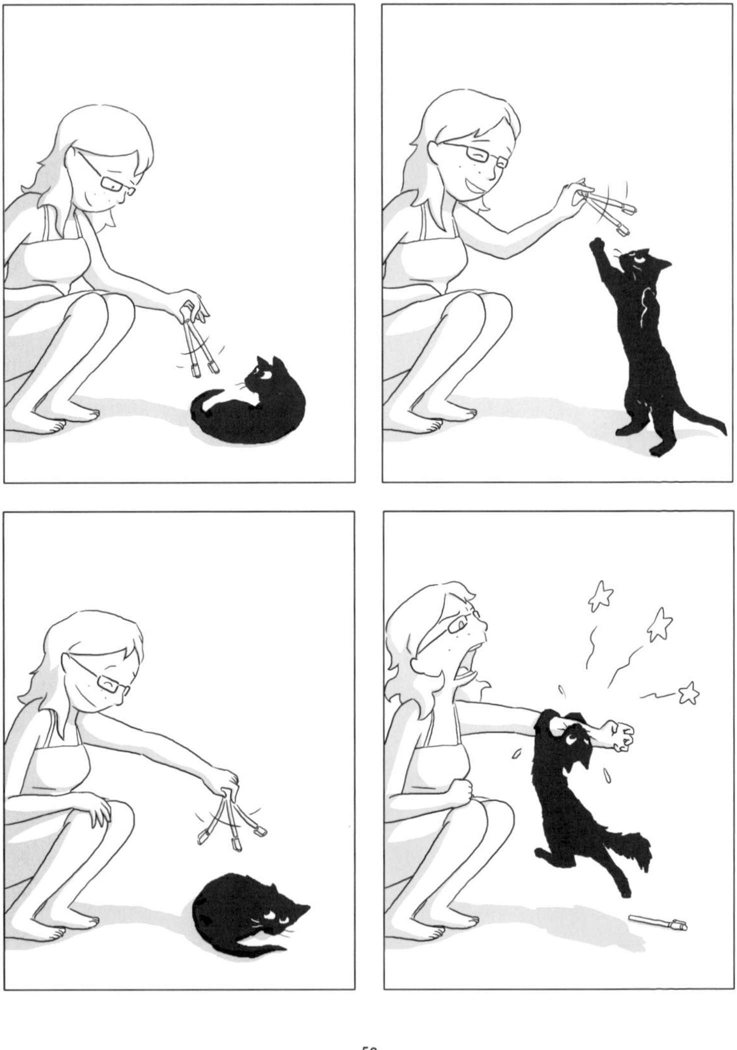

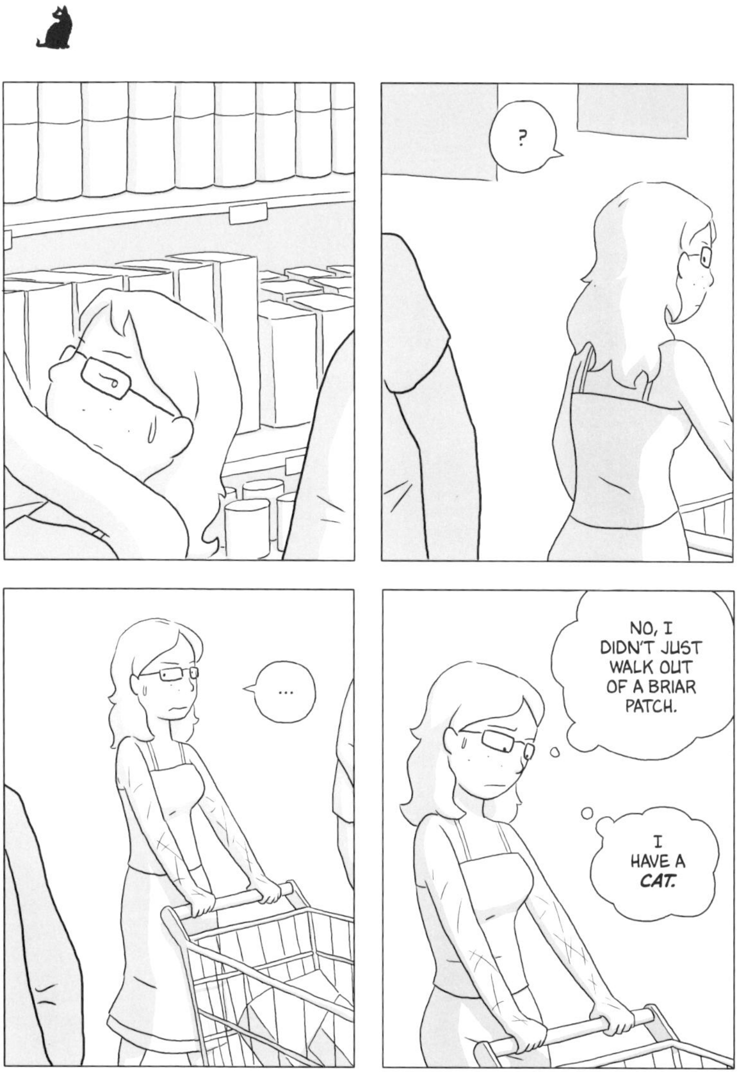
?
...
NO, I DIDN'T JUST WALK OUT OF A BRIAR PATCH.
I HAVE A *CAT.*

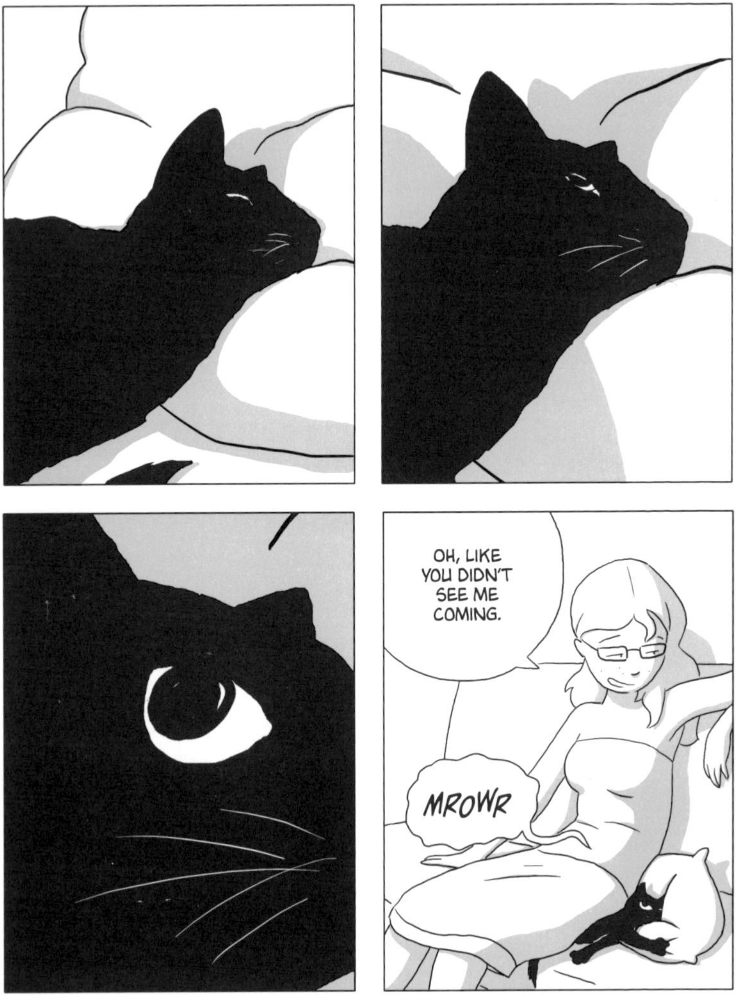
OH, LIKE YOU DIDN'T SEE ME COMING.
MROWR

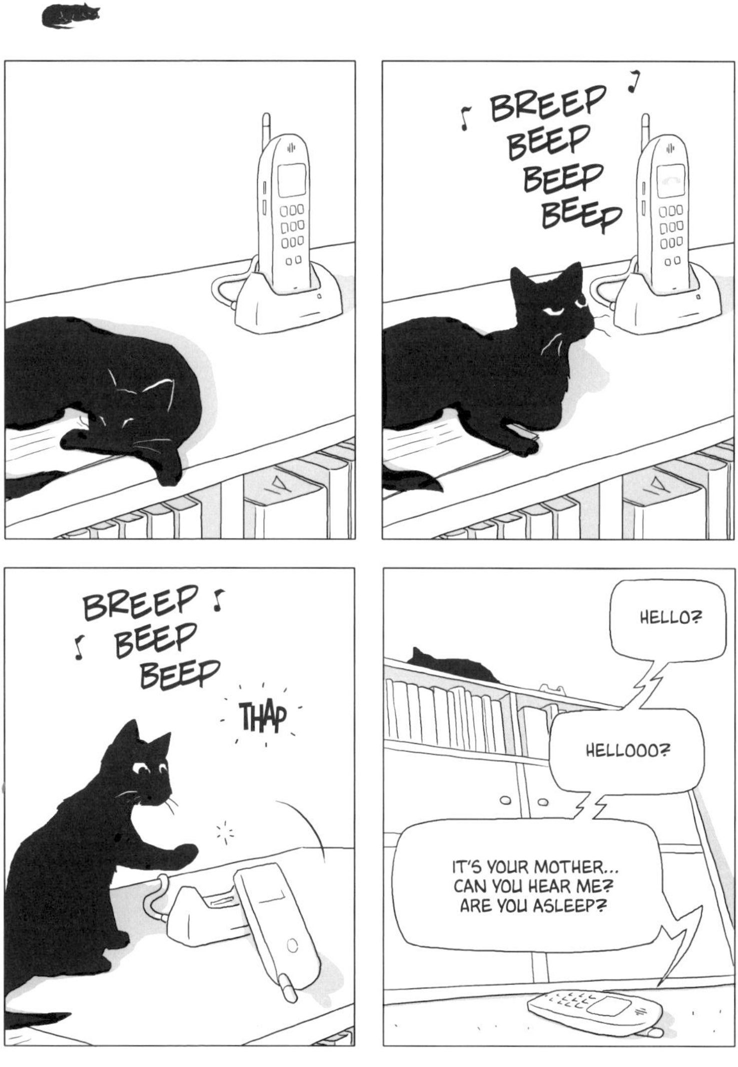
BREEP
BEEP
BEEP
BEEP
BREEP
BEEP
BEEP
THAP
HELLO?
HELLOOO?
IT'S YOUR MOTHER...
CAN YOU HEAR ME?
ARE YOU ASLEEP?

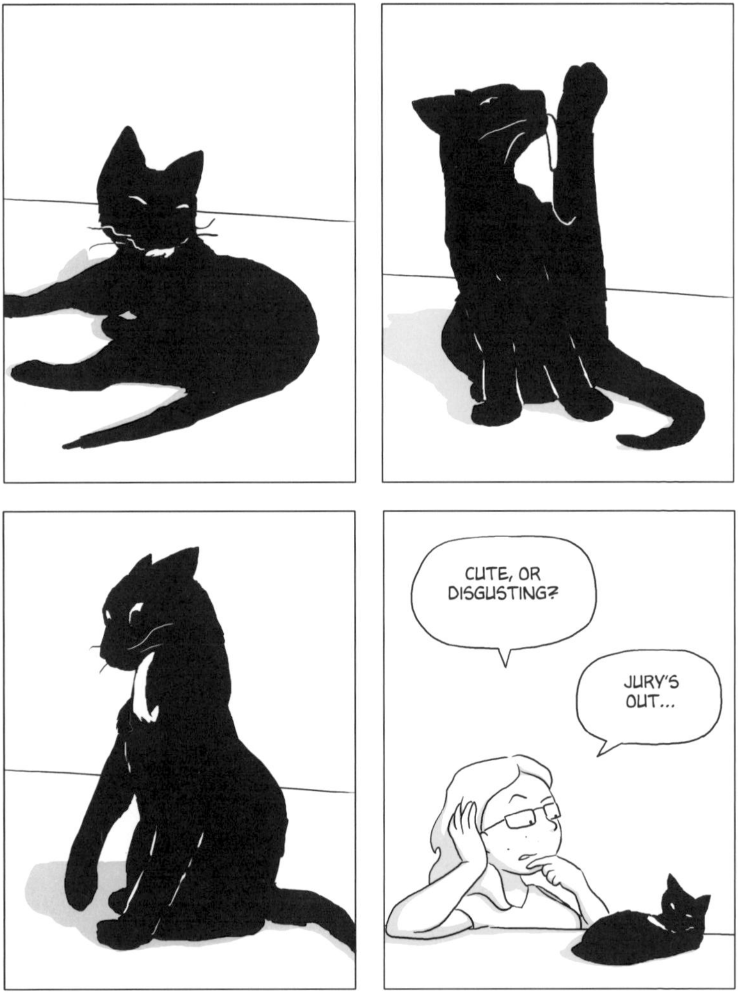
CUTE, OR DISGUSTING?
JURY'S OUT...

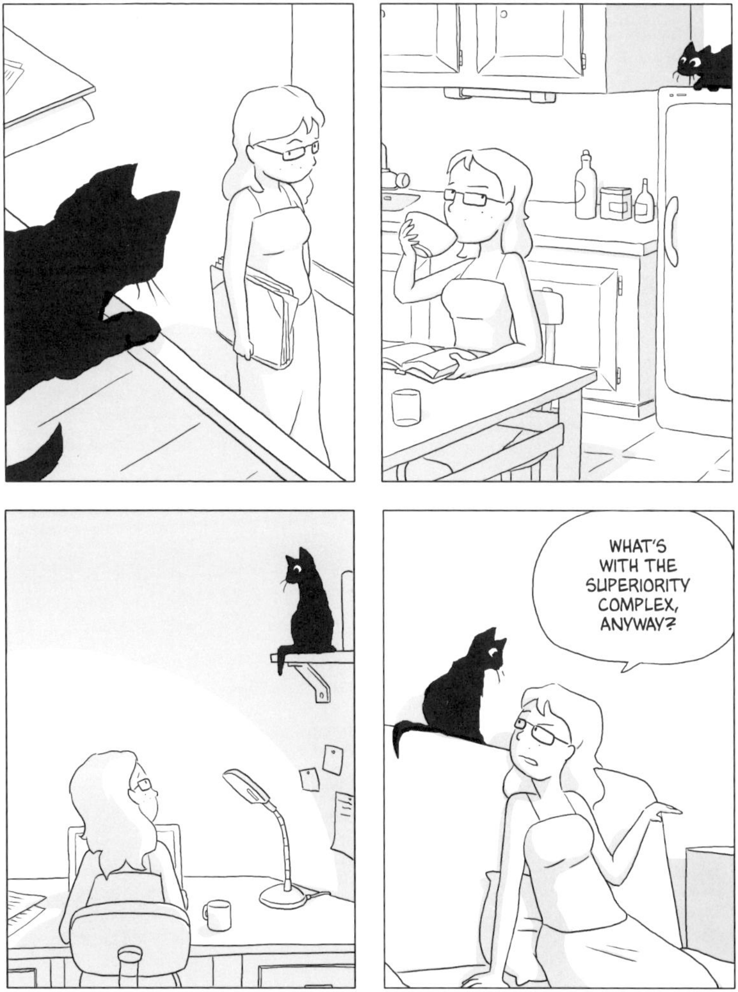
WHAT'S WITH THE SUPERIORITY COMPLEX, ANYWAY?

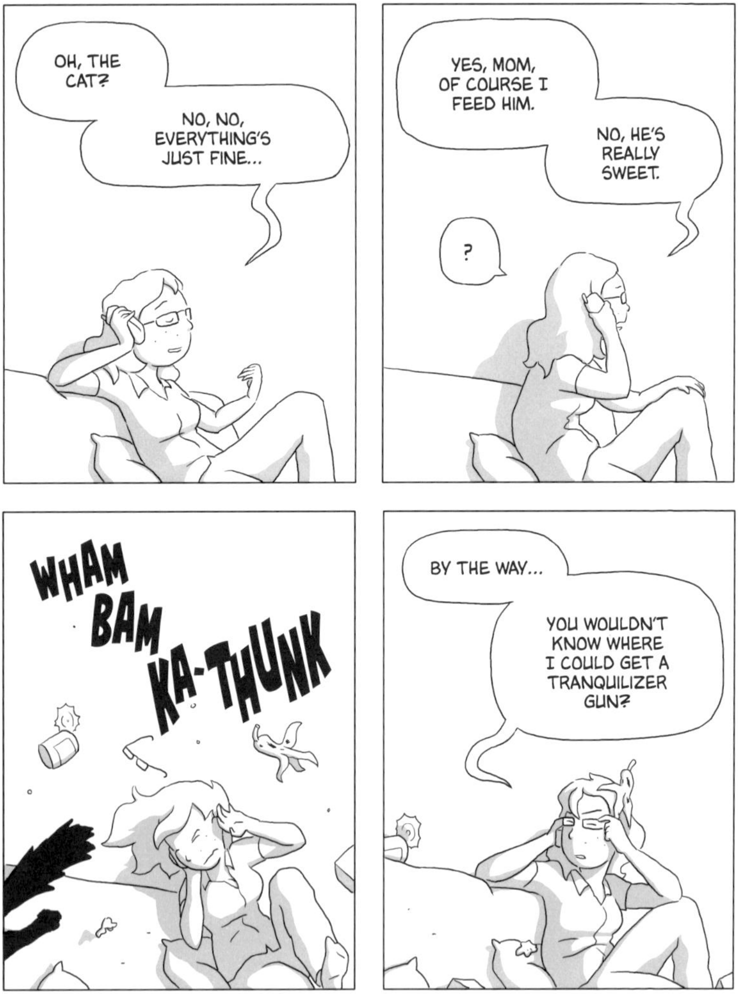
OH, THE CAT?
NO, NO, EVERYTHING'S JUST FINE...
YES, MOM, OF COURSE I FEED HIM.
NO, HE'S REALLY SWEET.
?
WHAM
BAM
KA-THUNK
BY THE WAY...
YOU WOULDN'T KNOW WHERE I COULD GET A TRANQUILIZER GUN?

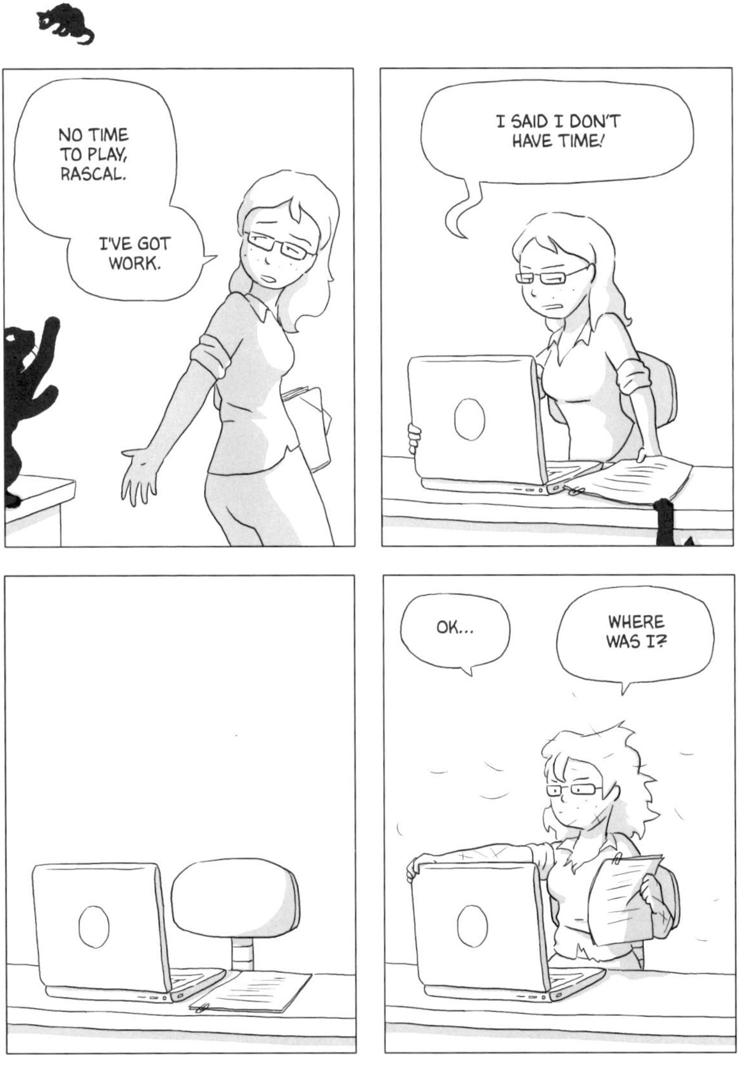
NO TIME TO PLAY, RASCAL.
I'VE GOT WORK.
I SAID I DON'T HAVE TIME!
OK...
WHERE WAS I?

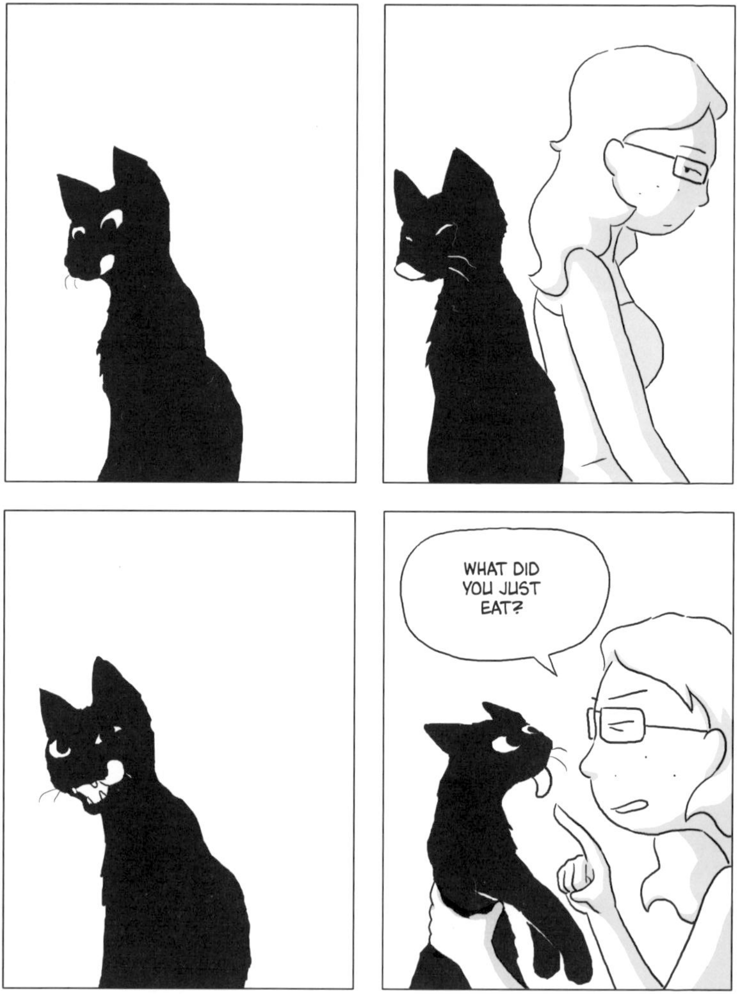
WHAT DID YOU JUST EAT?

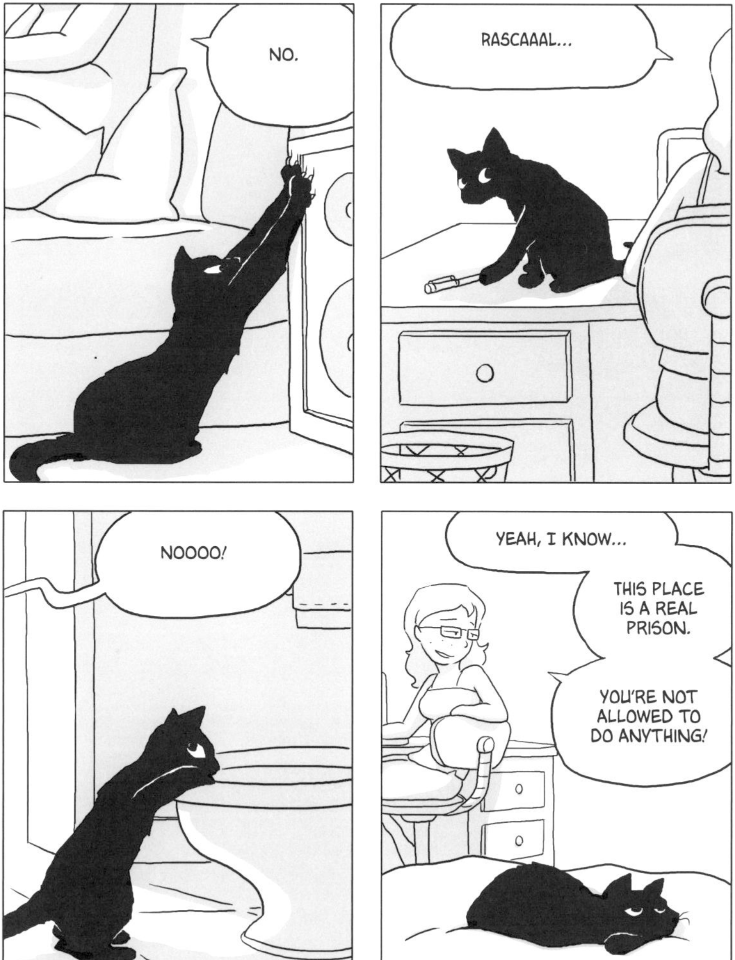
NO.
RASCAAAL...
NOOOO!
YEAH, I KNOW...
THIS PLACE IS A REAL PRISON.
YOU'RE NOT ALLOWED TO DO ANYTHING!

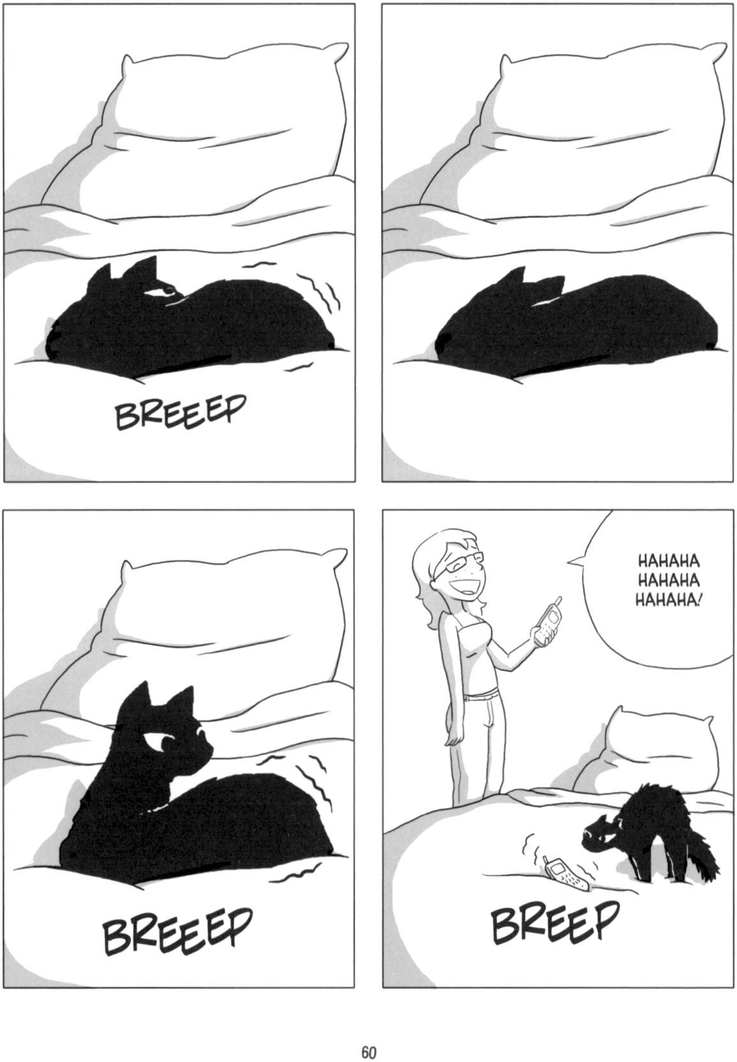
BREEEP
BREEEP
HAHAHA
HAHAHA
HAHAHA!
BREEP

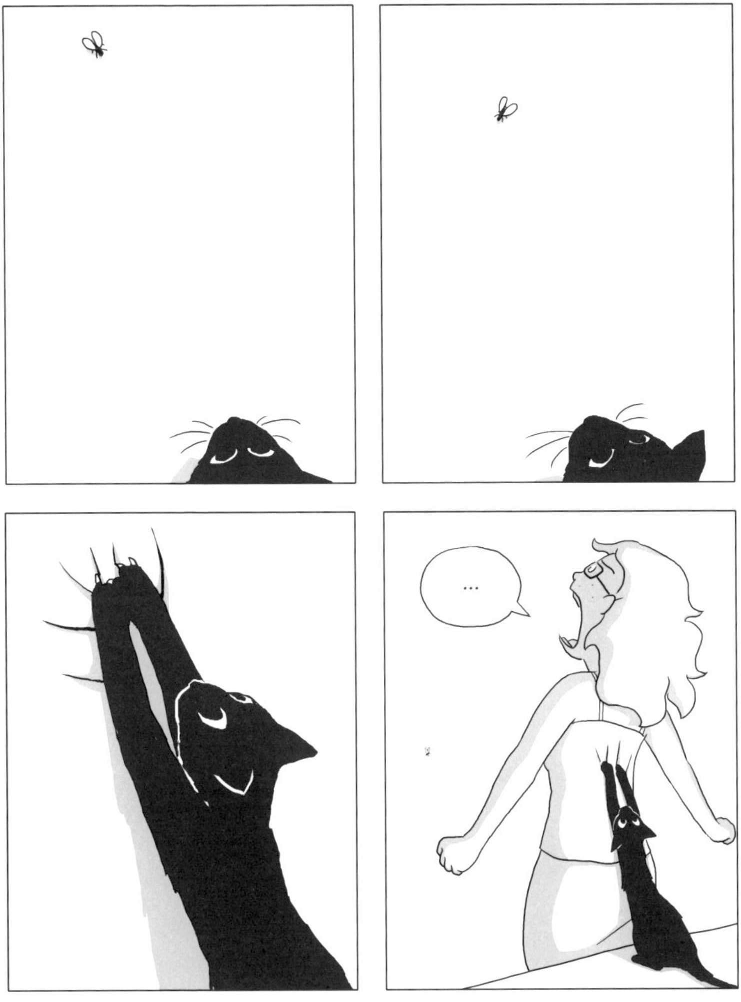
...

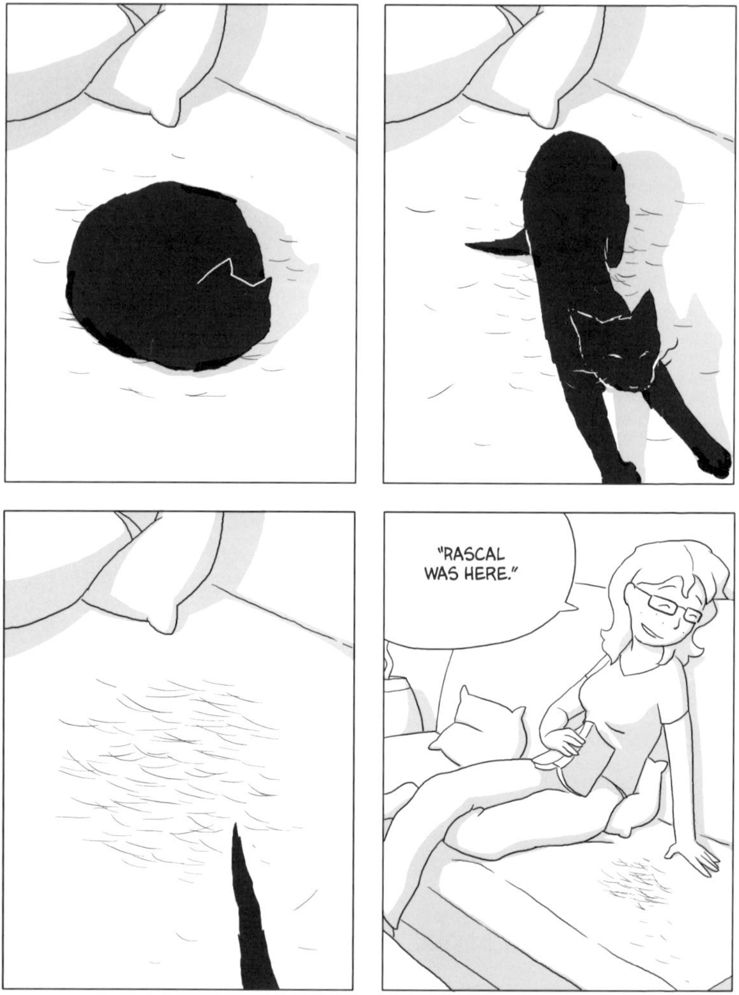
"RASCAL WAS HERE."

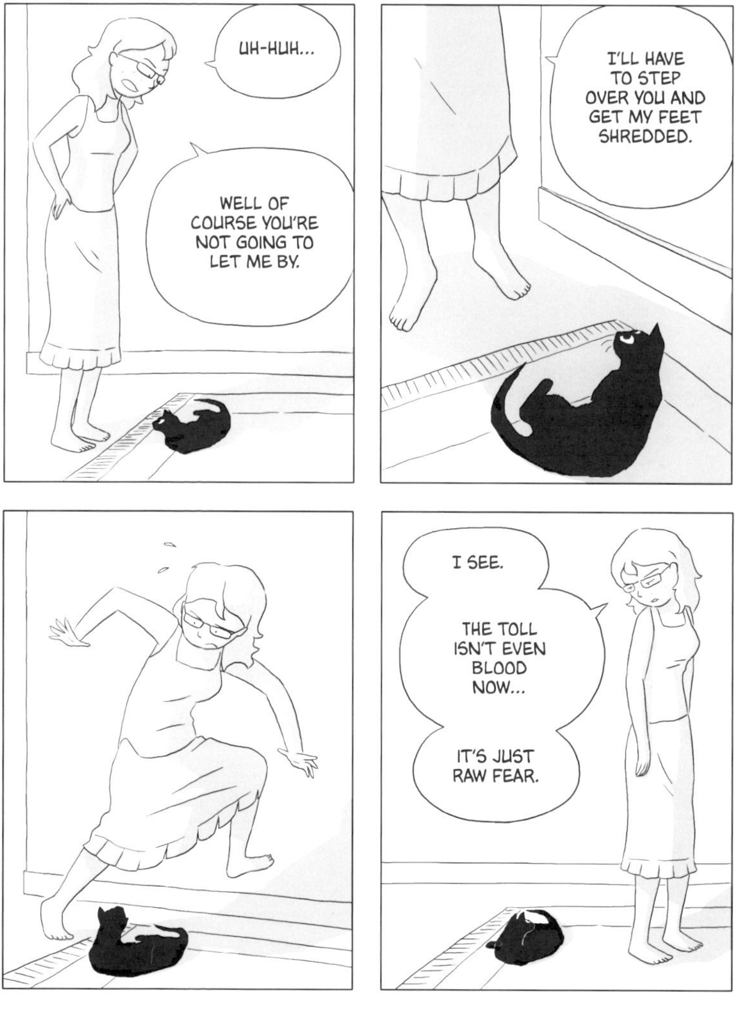
UH-HUH...
WELL OF COURSE YOU'RE NOT GOING TO LET ME BY.
I'LL HAVE TO STEP OVER YOU AND GET MY FEET SHREDDED.
I SEE.
THE TOLL ISN'T EVEN BLOOD NOW...
IT'S JUST RAW FEAR.

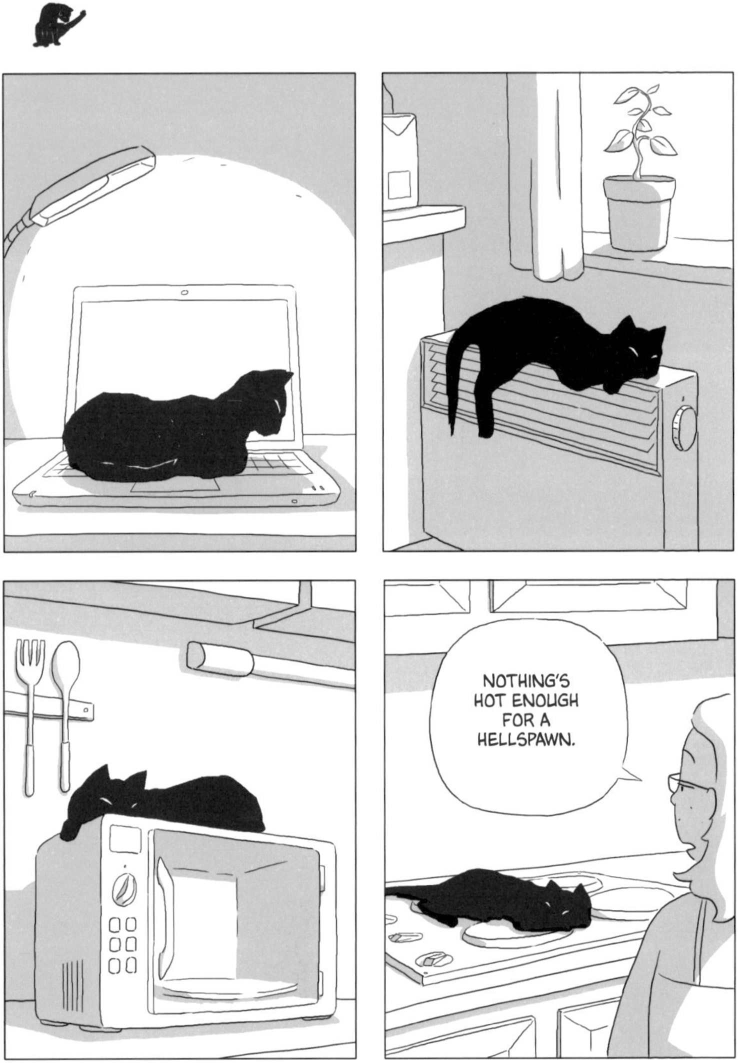
NOTHING'S HOT ENOUGH FOR A HELLSPAWN.

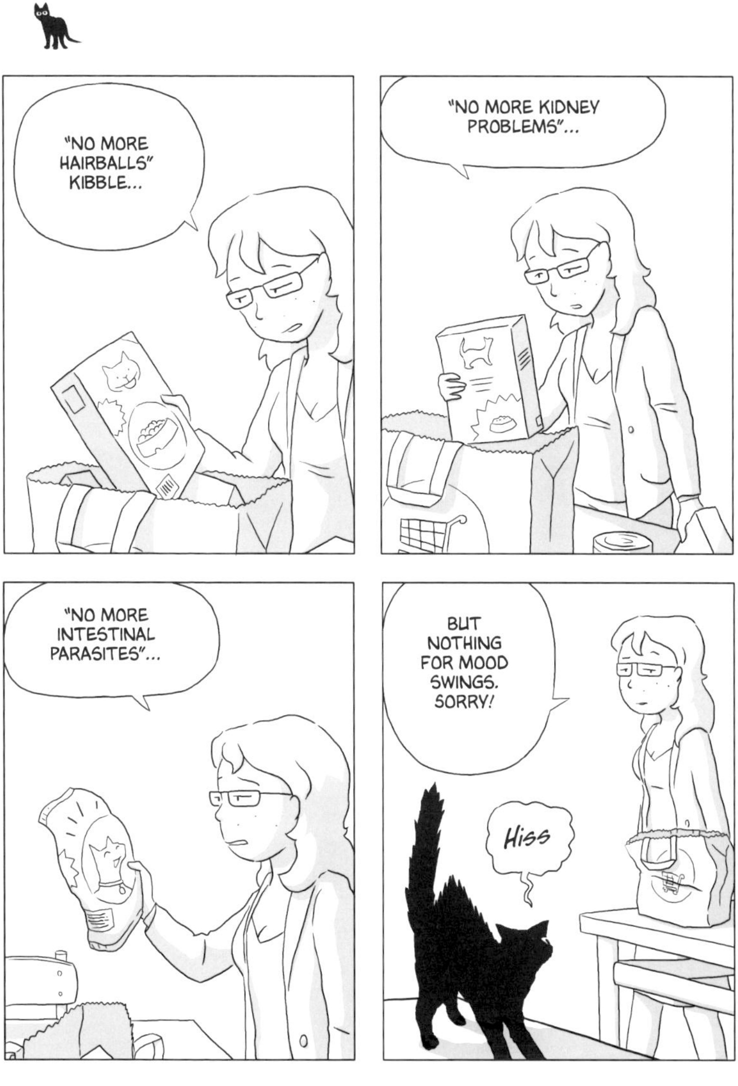
"NO MORE HAIRBALLS" KIBBLE...
"NO MORE KIDNEY PROBLEMS"...
"NO MORE INTESTINAL PARASITES"...
BUT NOTHING FOR MOOD SWINGS. SORRY!
Hiss

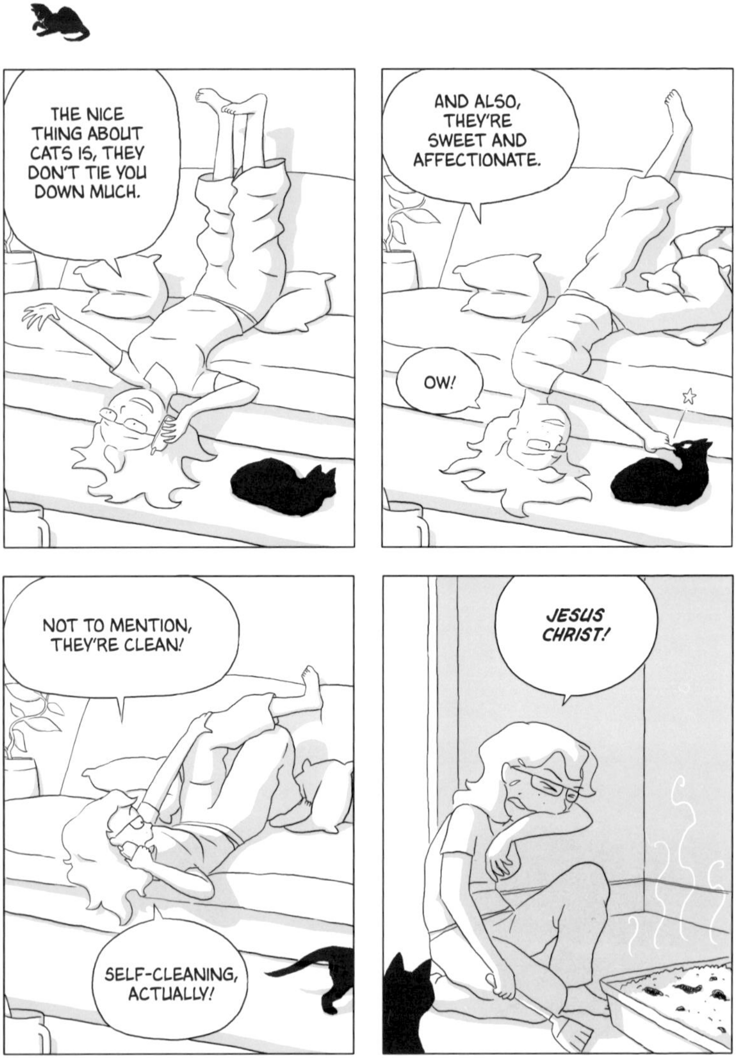
THE NICE THING ABOUT CATS IS, THEY DON'T TIE YOU DOWN MUCH.
AND ALSO, THEY'RE SWEET AND AFFECTIONATE.
OW!
NOT TO MENTION, THEY'RE CLEAN!
SELF-CLEANING, ACTUALLY!
JESUS CHRIST!

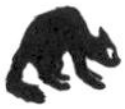

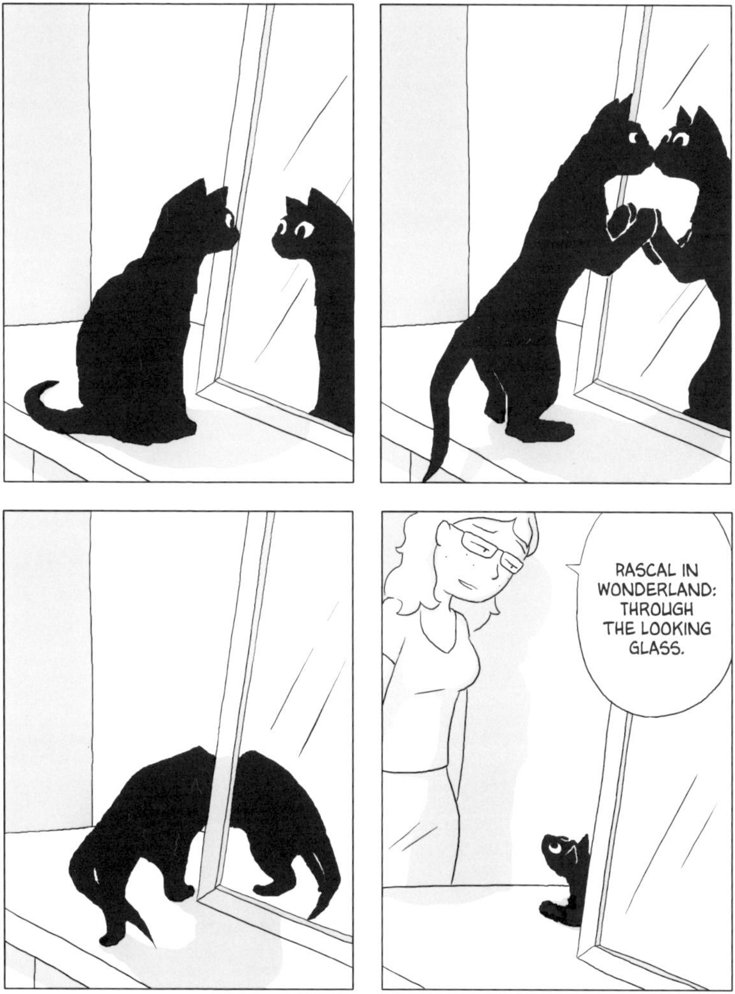
RASCAL IN WONDERLAND: THROUGH THE LOOKING GLASS.

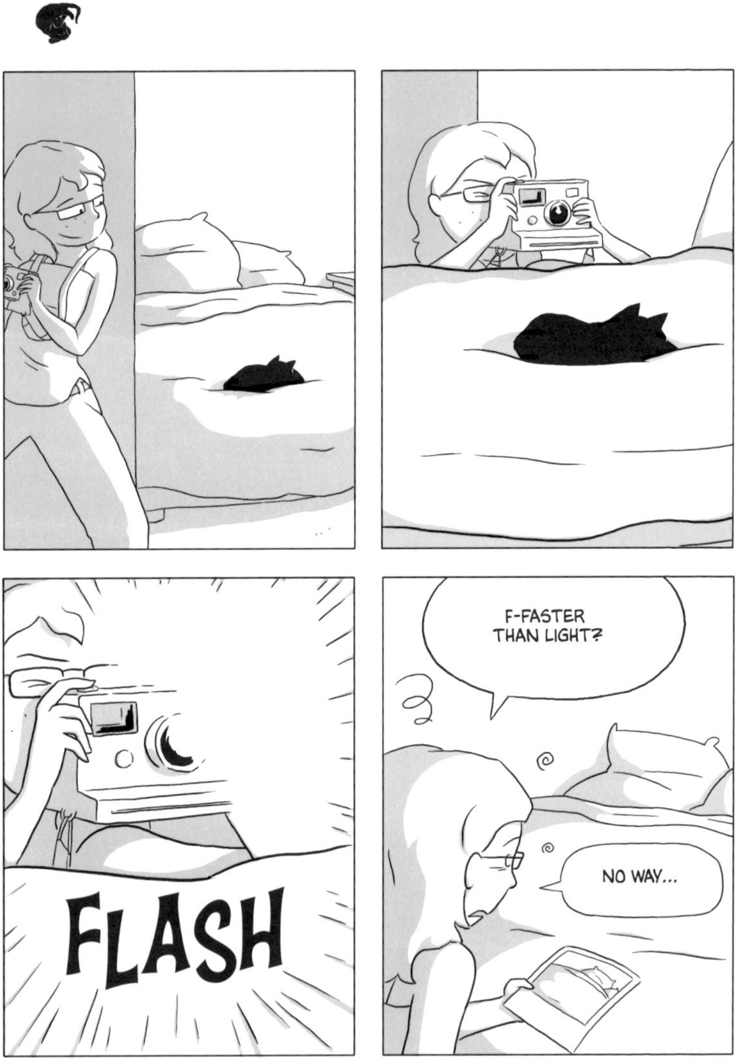
FLASH
F-FASTER THAN LIGHT?
NO WAY...

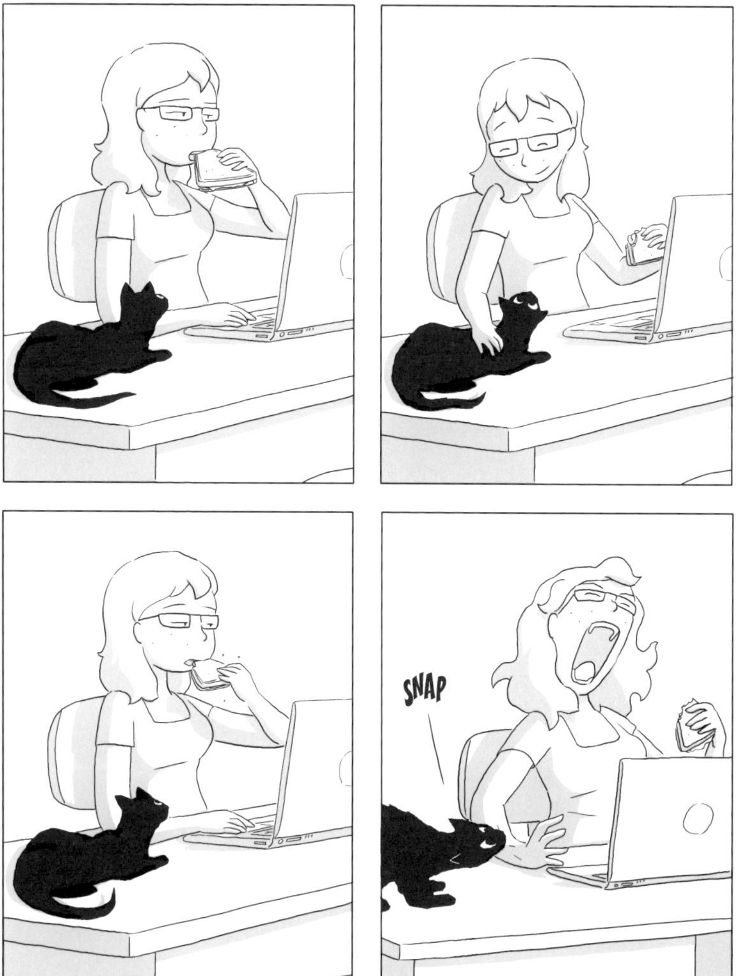
SNAP

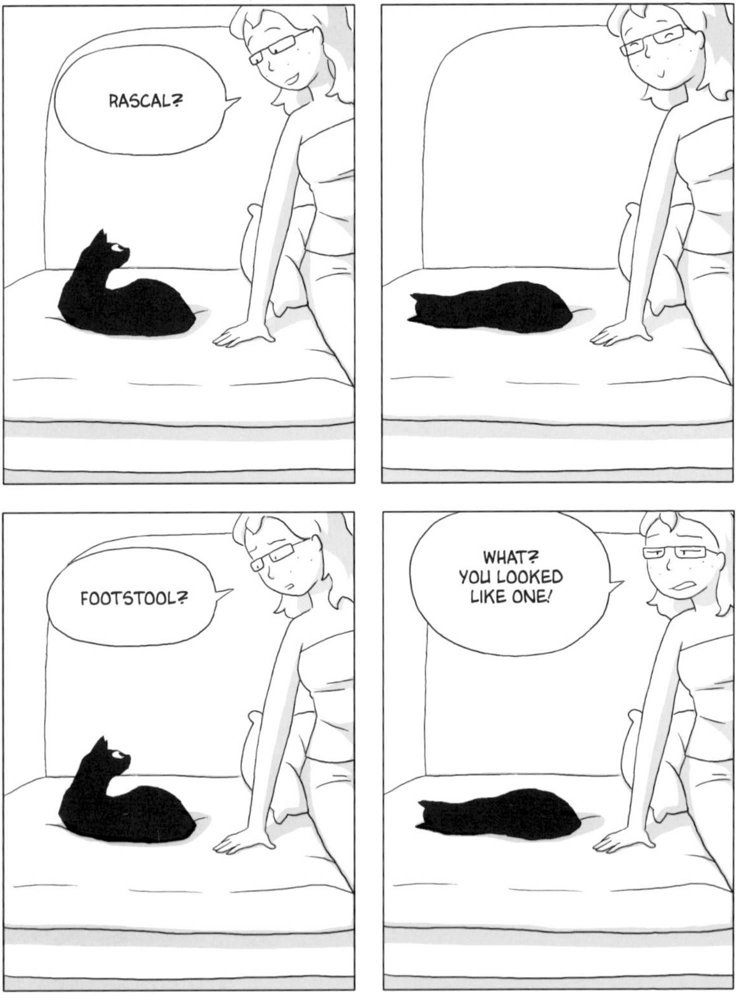
RASCAL?
FOOTSTOOL?
WHAT? YOU LOOKED LIKE ONE!

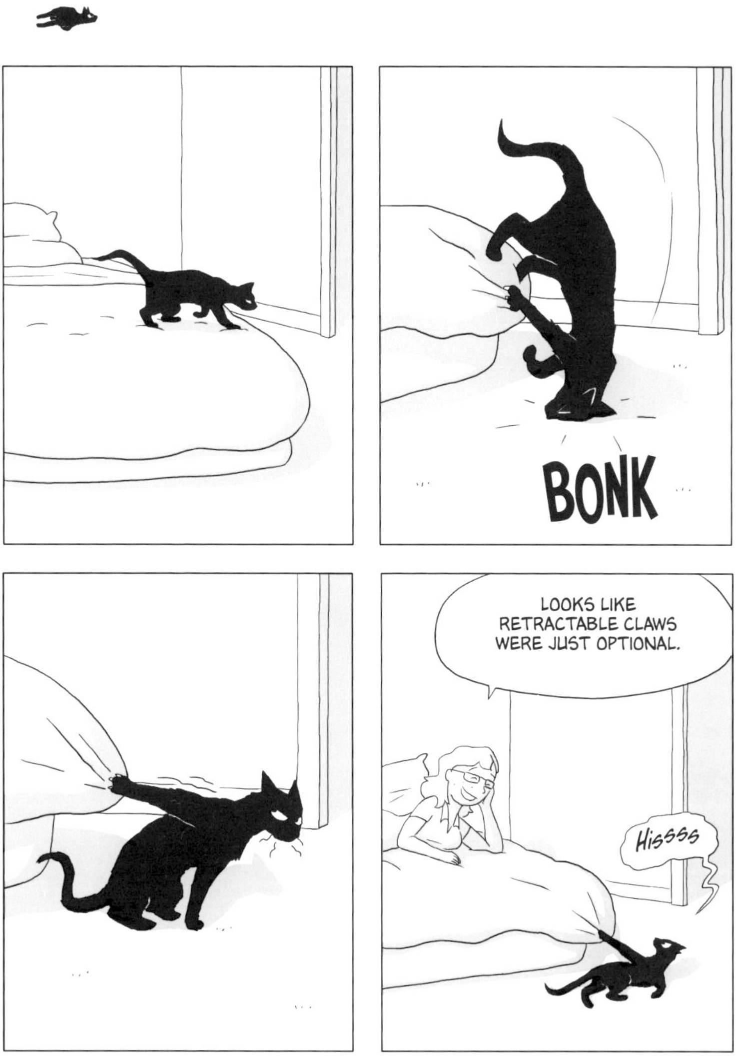
BONK
LOOKS LIKE RETRACTABLE CLAWS WERE JUST OPTIONAL.
Hissss

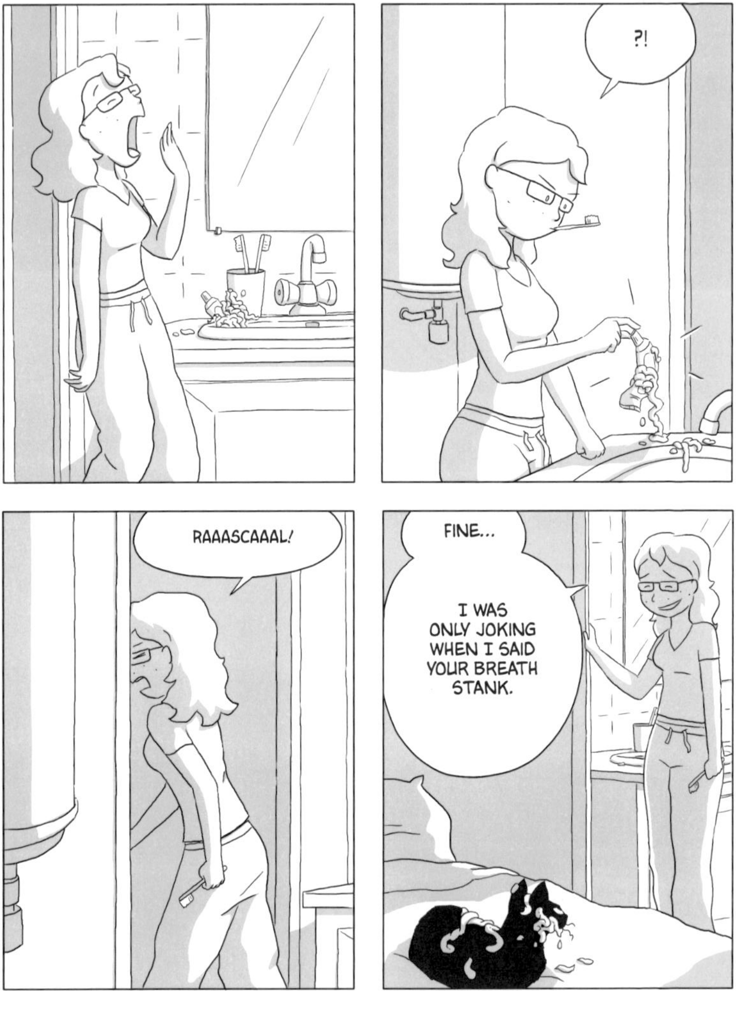
?!
RAAASCAAAL!
FINE...
I WAS ONLY JOKING WHEN I SAID YOUR BREATH STANK.

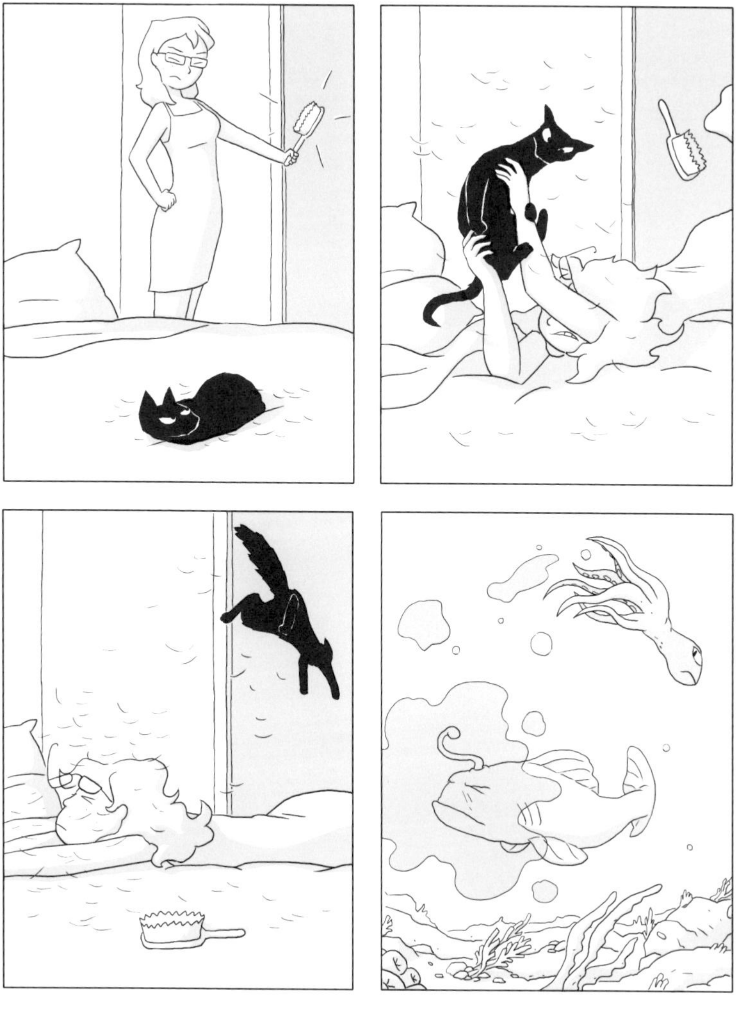

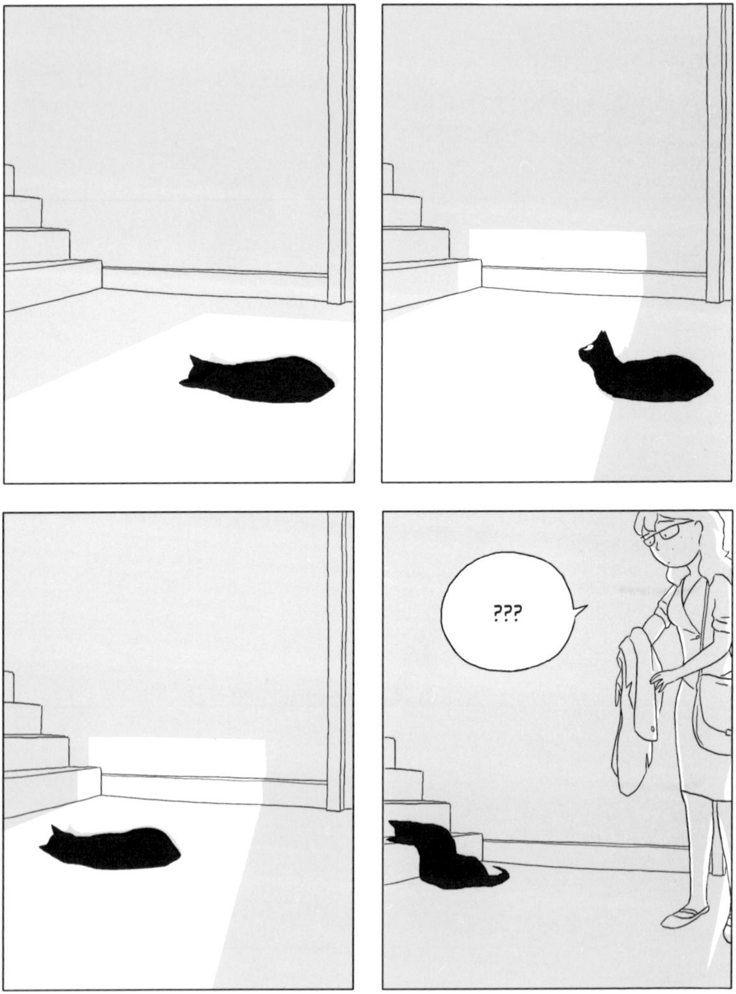
???

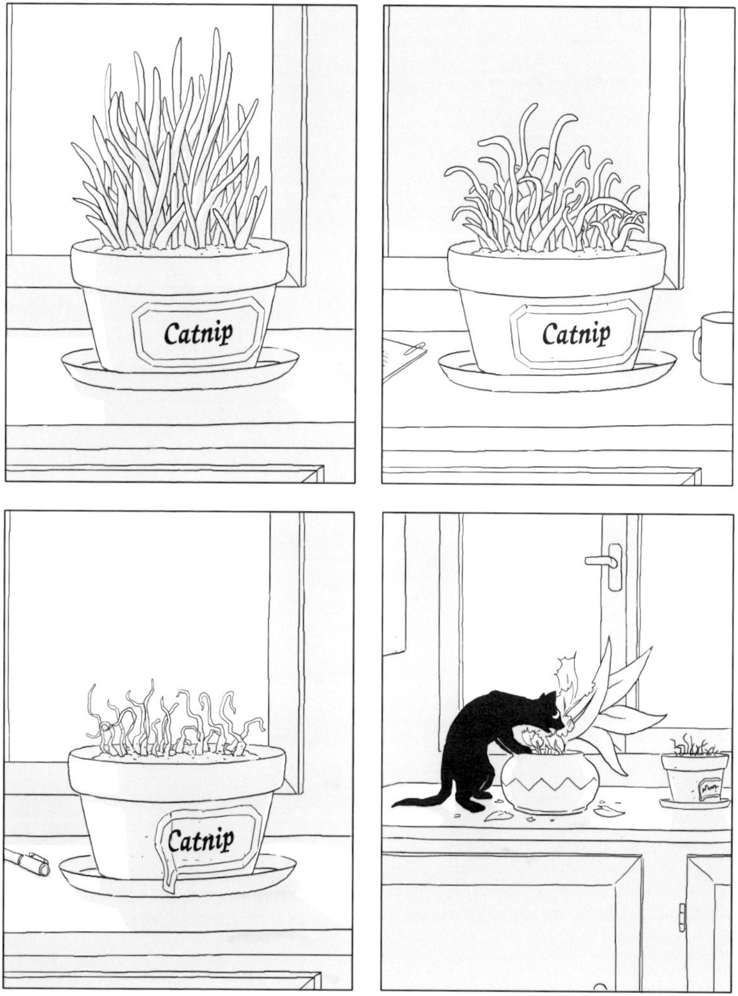
Catnip
Catnip
Catnip

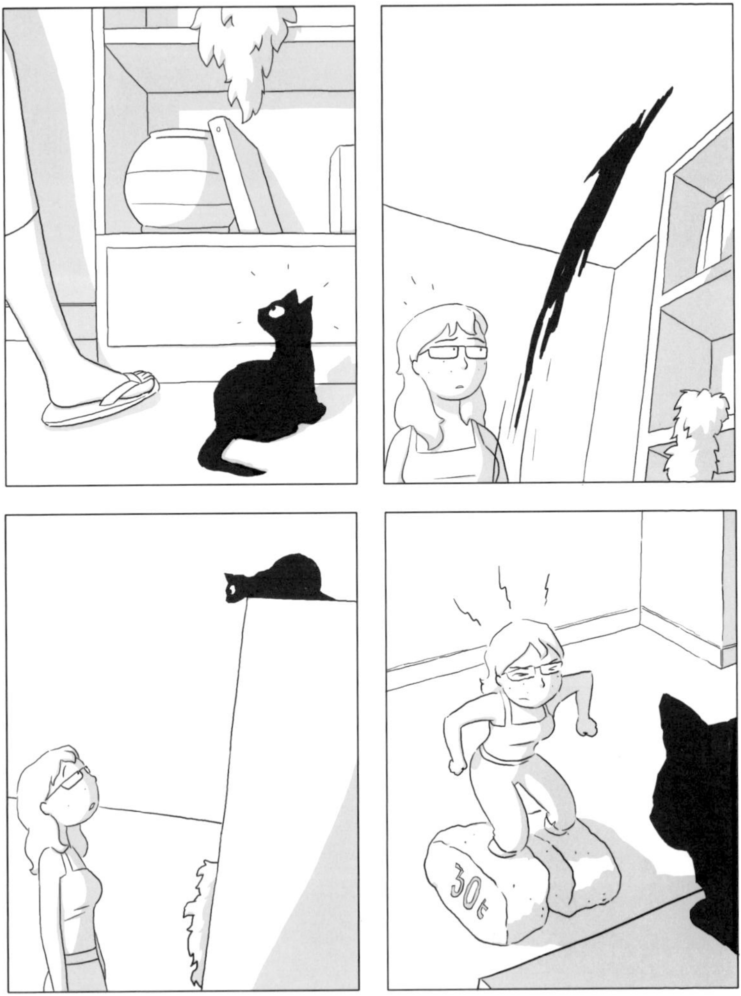
30t

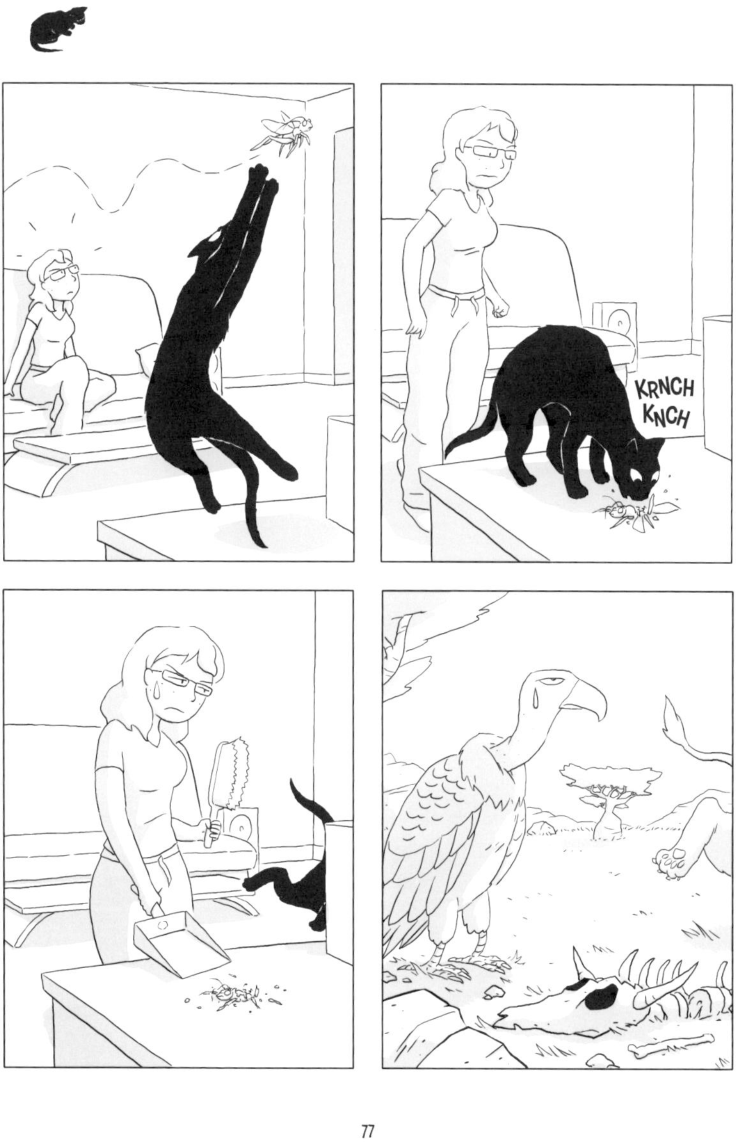
KRNCH
KNCH

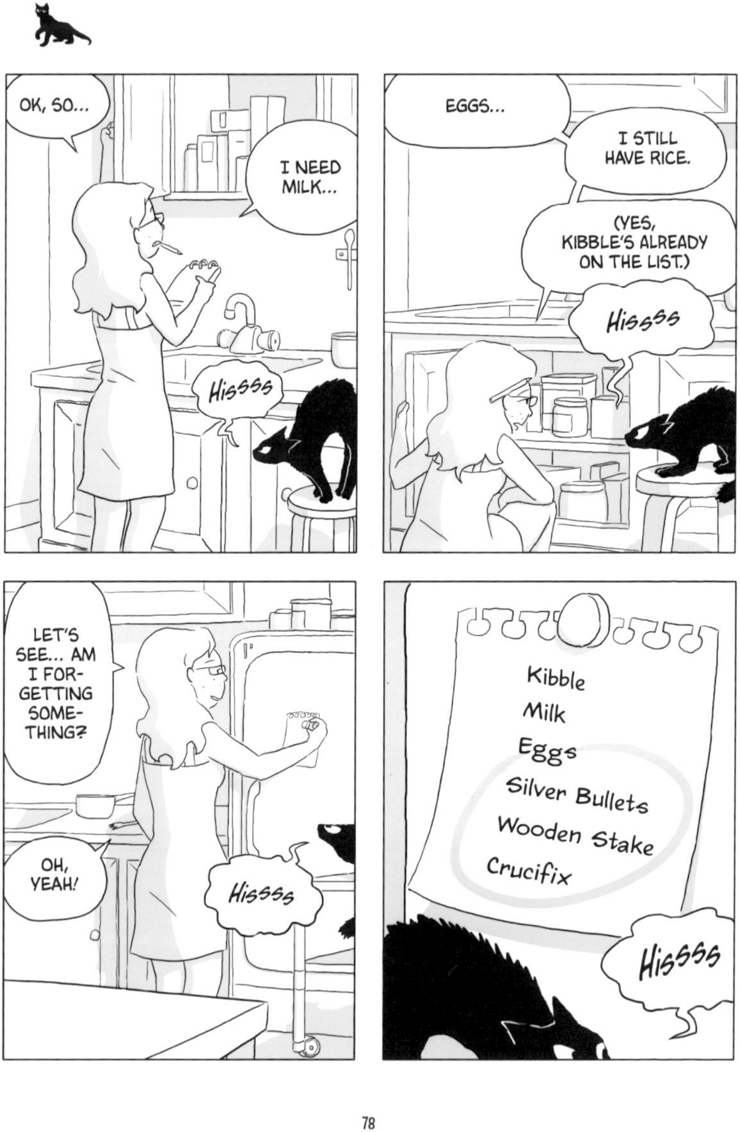
OK, SO...
I NEED MILK...
Hissss
EGGS...
I STILL HAVE RICE.
(YES, KIBBLE'S ALREADY ON THE LIST.)
Hissss
LET'S SEE... AM I FOR-GETTING SOME-THING?
OH, YEAH!
Hissss
Kibble
Milk
Eggs
Silver Bullets
Wooden Stake
Crucifix
Hissss

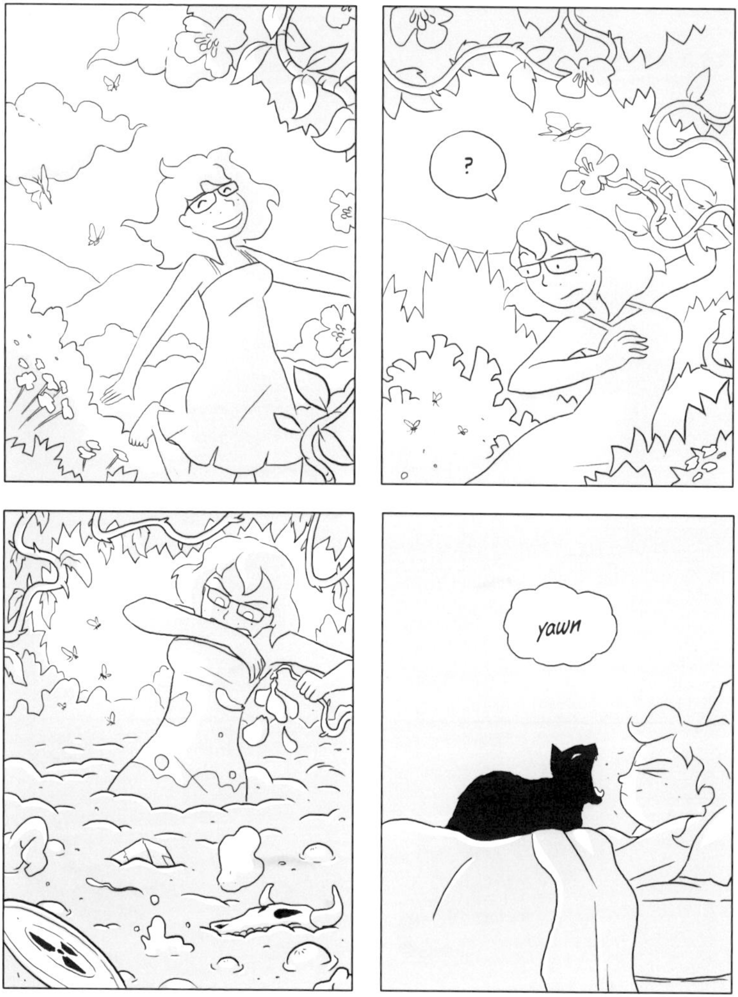
?
yawn

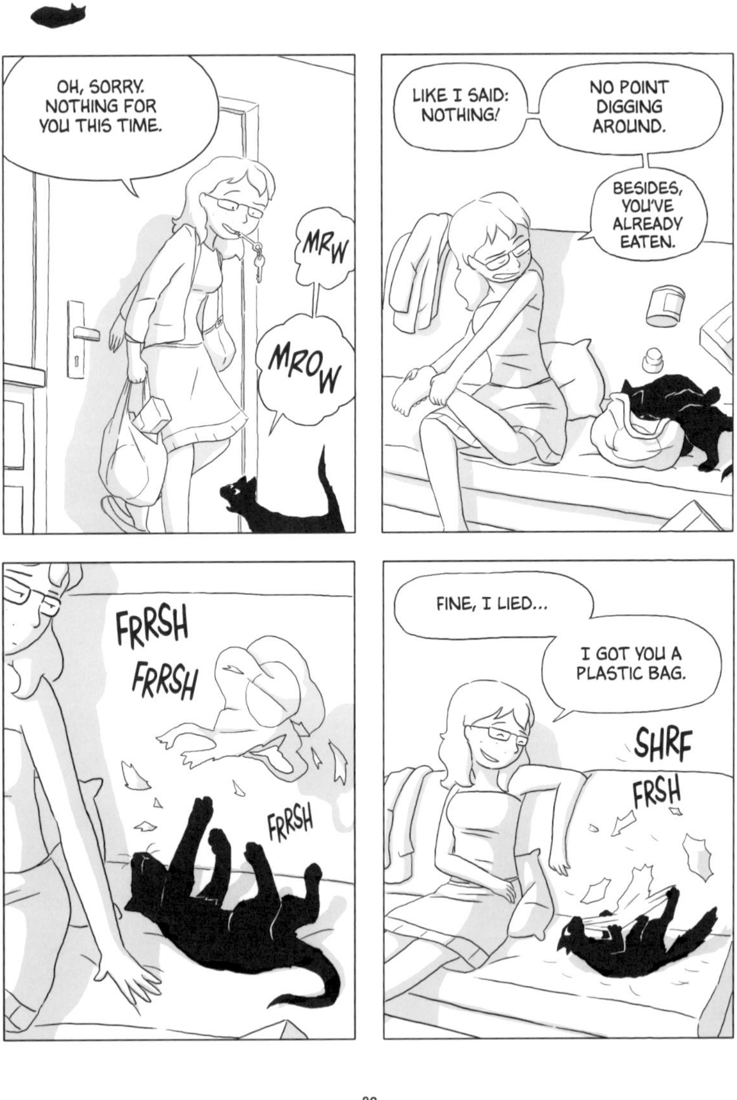
OH, SORRY. NOTHING FOR YOU THIS TIME.
MRW
MROW
LIKE I SAID: NOTHING!
NO POINT DIGGING AROUND.
BESIDES, YOU'VE ALREADY EATEN.
FRRSH
FRRSH
FRRSH
FINE, I LIED...
I GOT YOU A PLASTIC BAG.
SHRF
FRSH

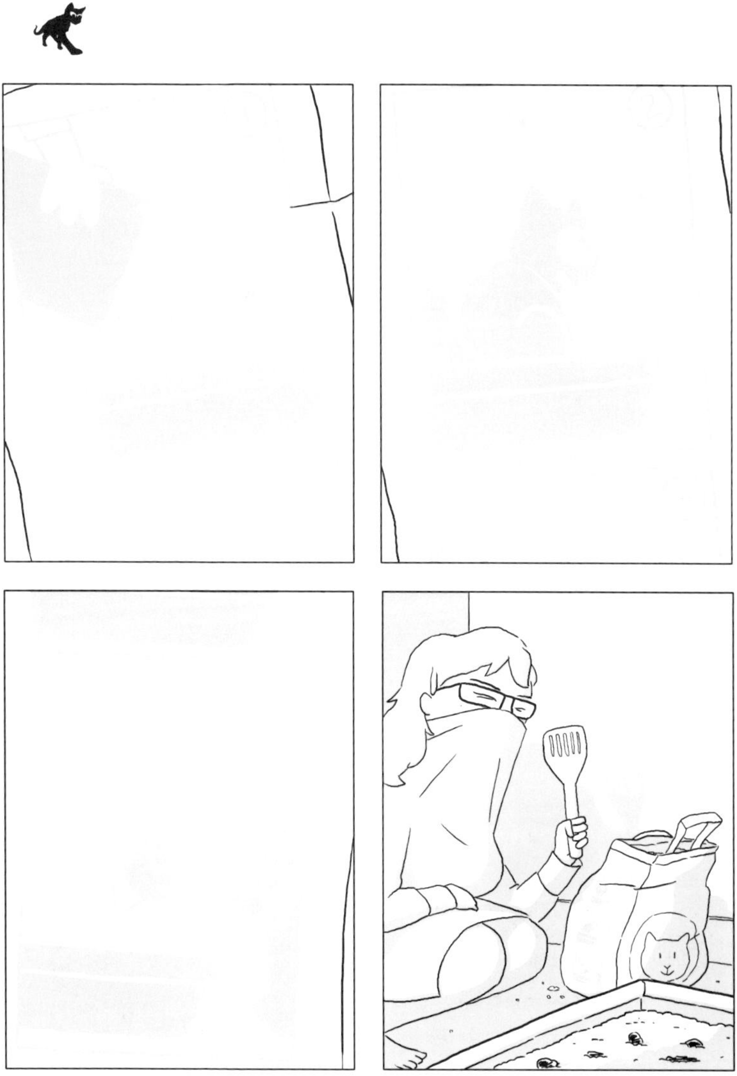

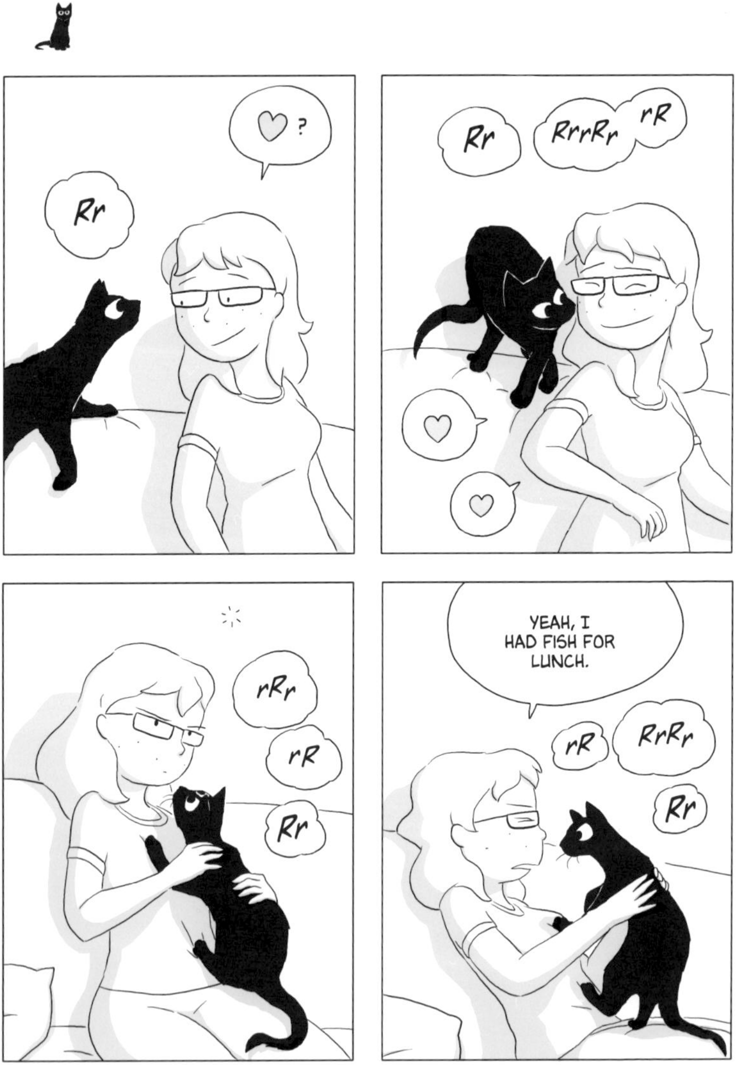
Rr
?
Rr
RrrRr
rR
rRr
rR
Rr
YEAH, I HAD FISH FOR LUNCH.
rR
RrRr
Rr

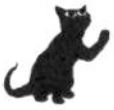

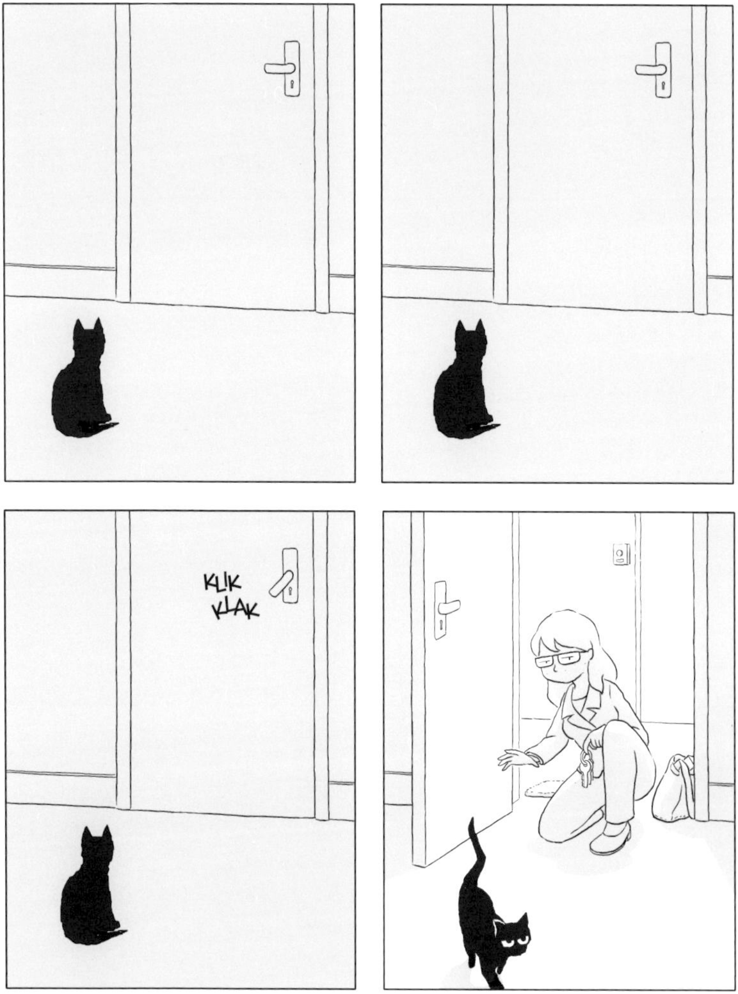
KLIK
KLAK

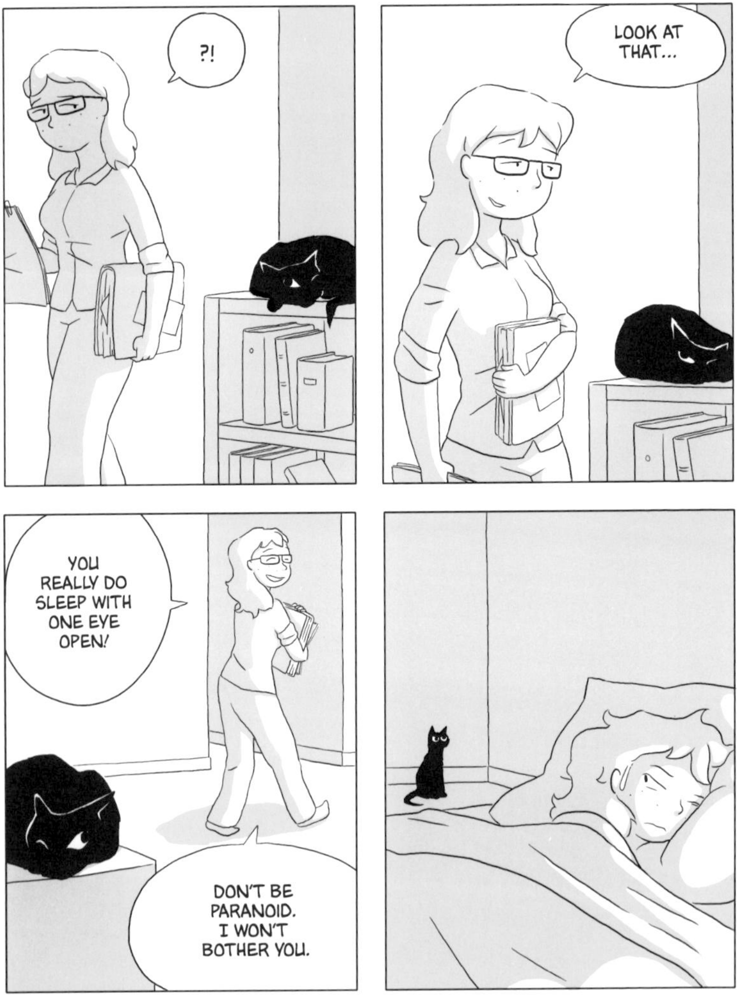
?!
LOOK AT THAT...
YOU REALLY DO SLEEP WITH ONE EYE OPEN!
DON'T BE PARANOID. I WON'T BOTHER YOU.

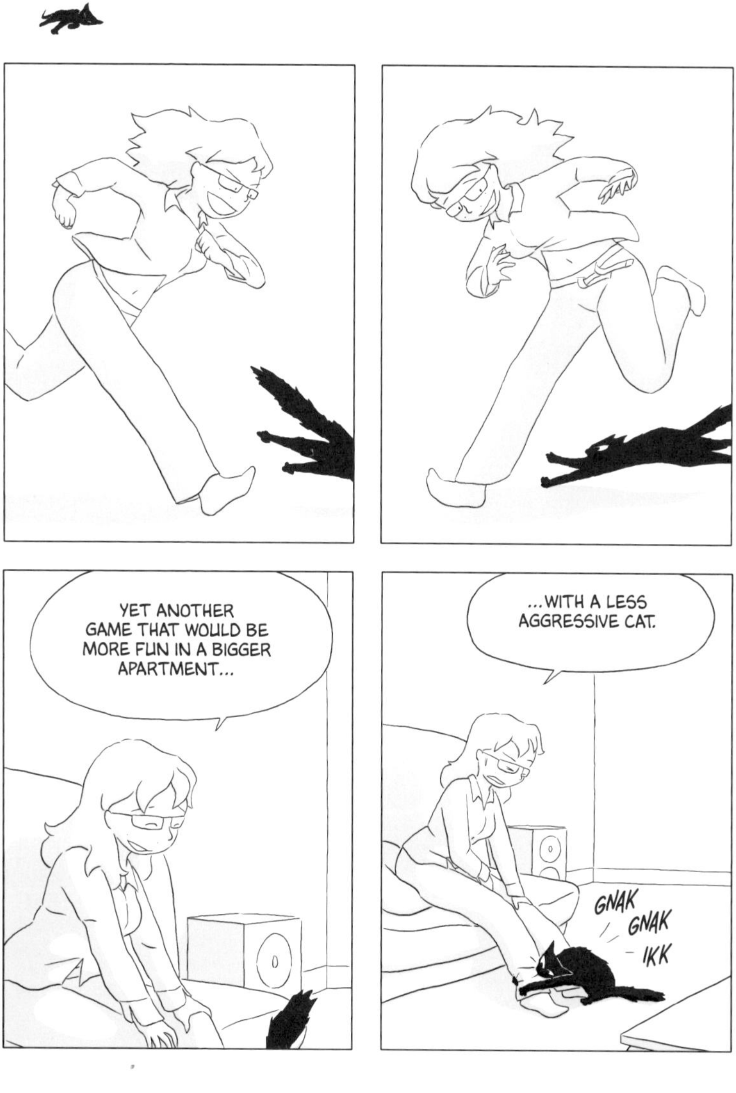
YET ANOTHER GAME THAT WOULD BE MORE FUN IN A BIGGER APARTMENT...
...WITH A LESS AGGRESSIVE CAT.
GNAK
GNAK
IKK

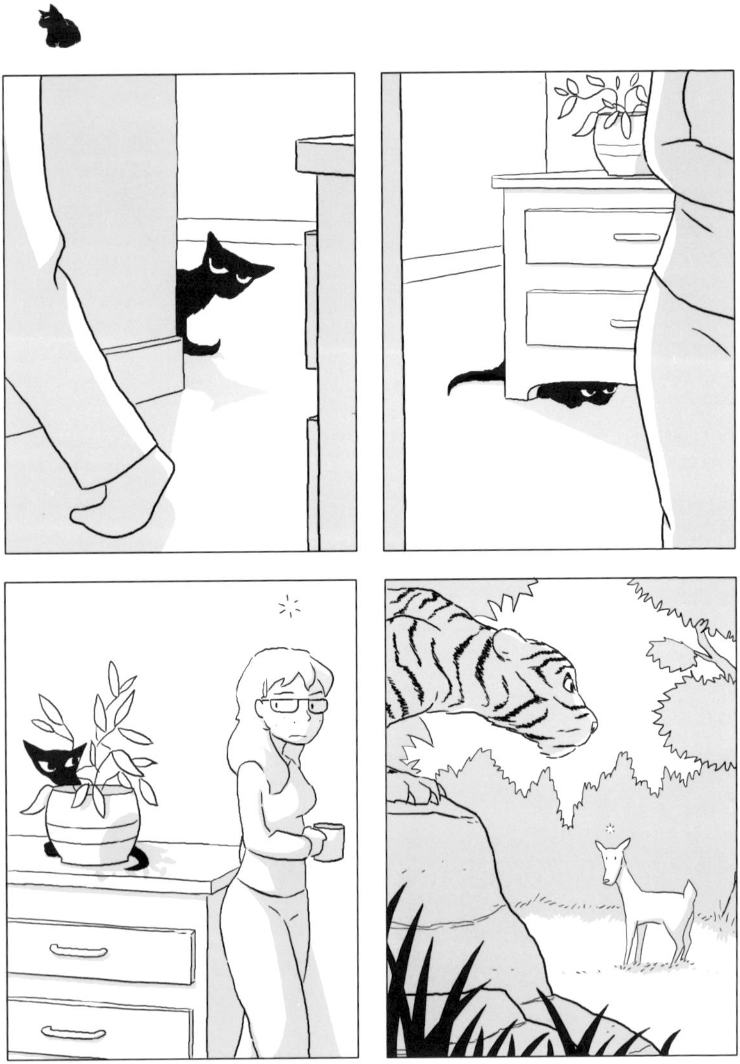

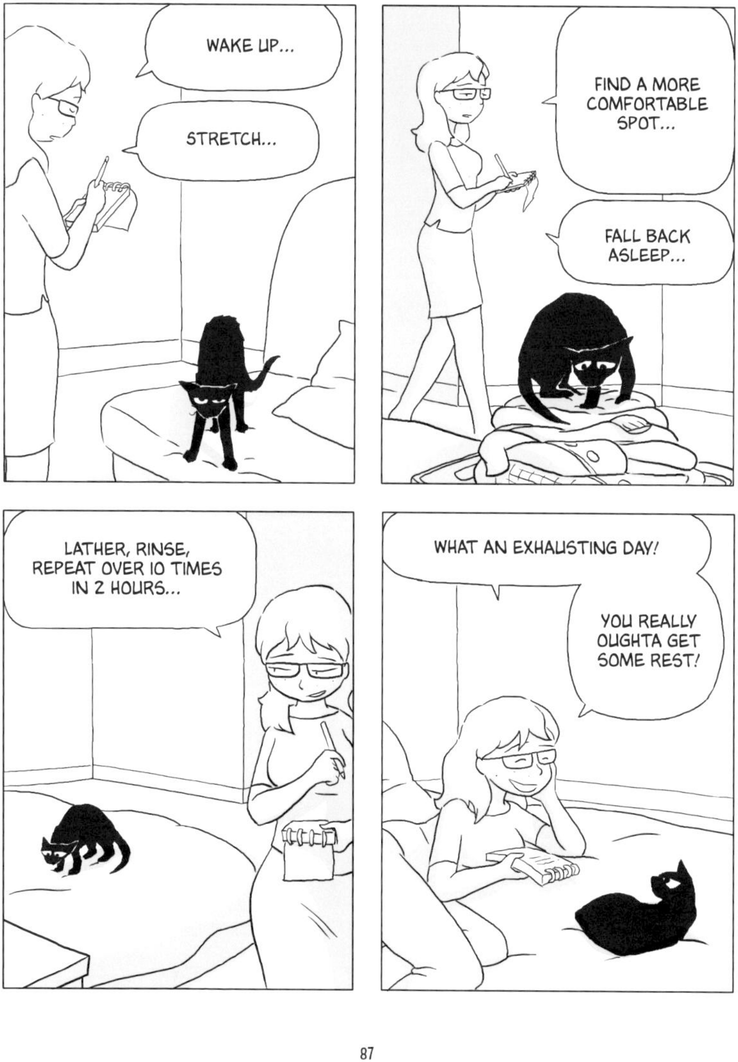
WAKE UP...
STRETCH...
FIND A MORE COMFORTABLE SPOT...
FALL BACK ASLEEP...
LATHER, RINSE, REPEAT OVER 10 TIMES IN 2 HOURS...
WHAT AN EXHAUSTING DAY!
YOU REALLY OUGHTA GET SOME REST!

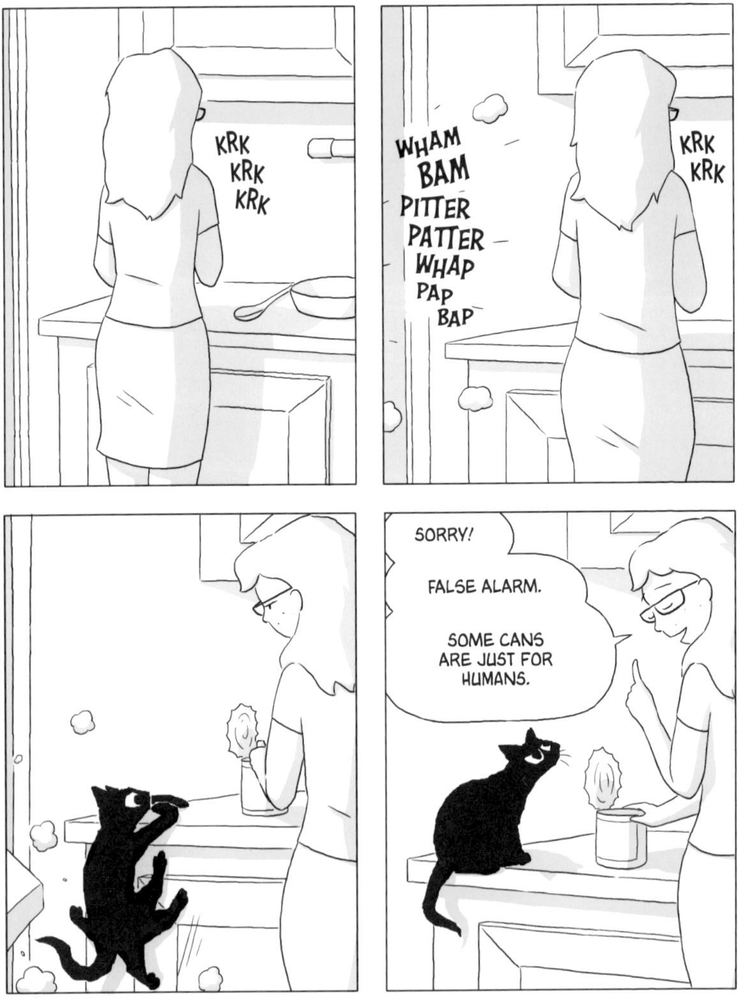
KRK KRK KRK
WHAM BAM PITTER PATTER WHAP PAP BAP
KRK KRK
SORRY!
FALSE ALARM.
SOME CANS ARE JUST FOR HUMANS.

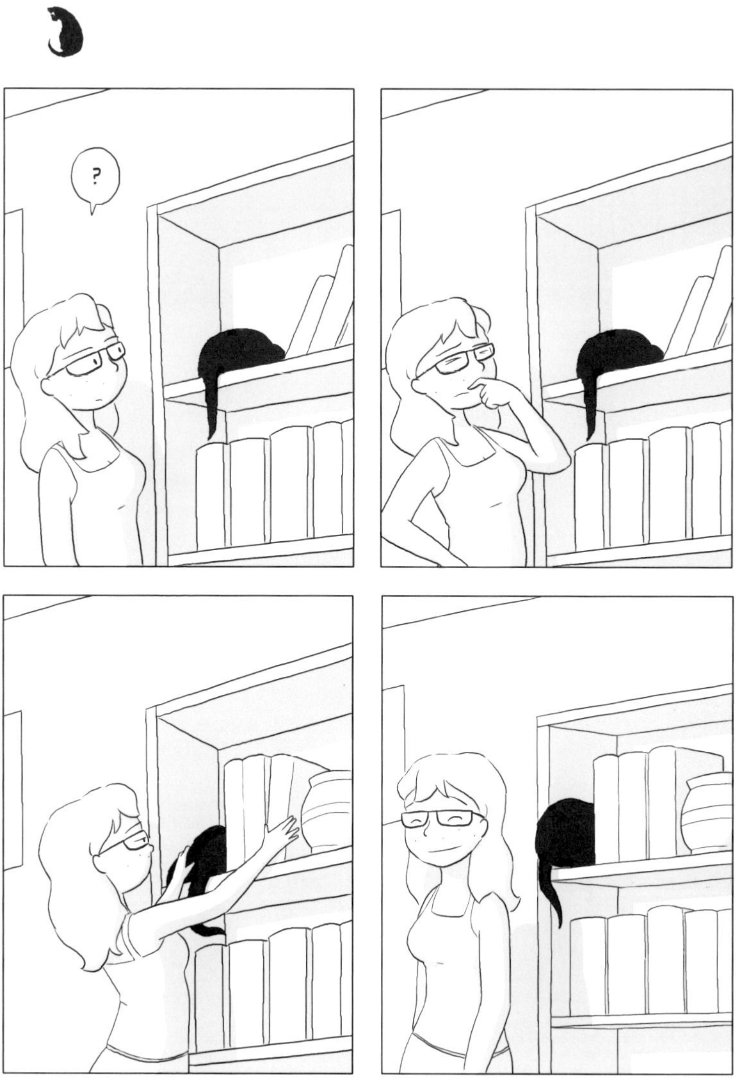
?

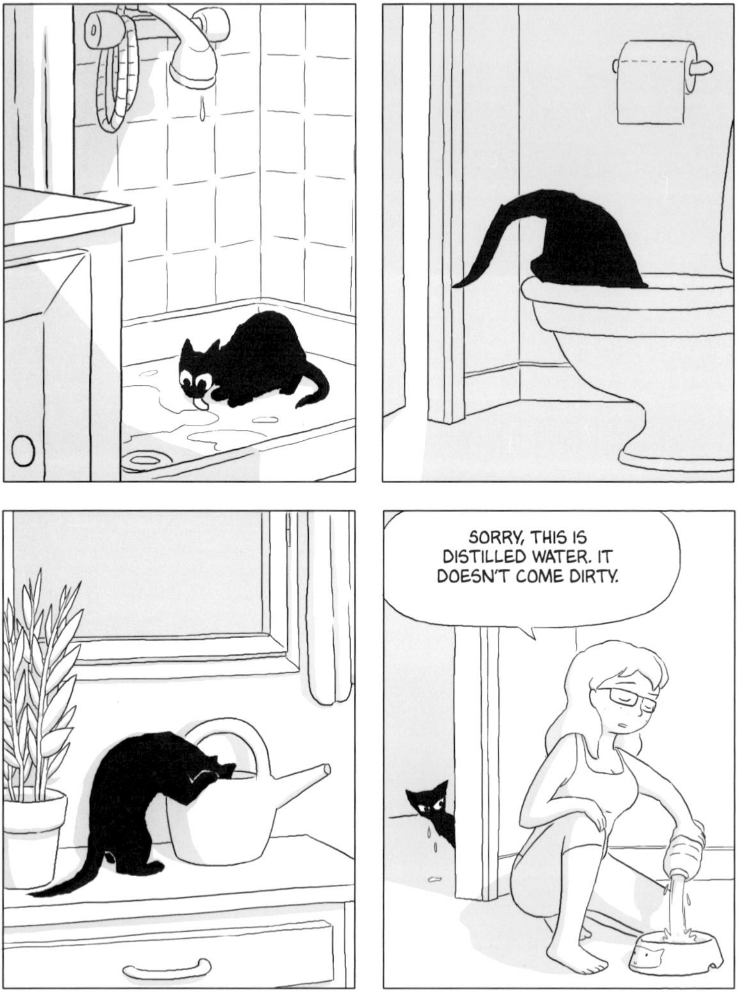
SORRY, THIS IS DISTILLED WATER. IT DOESN'T COME DIRTY.

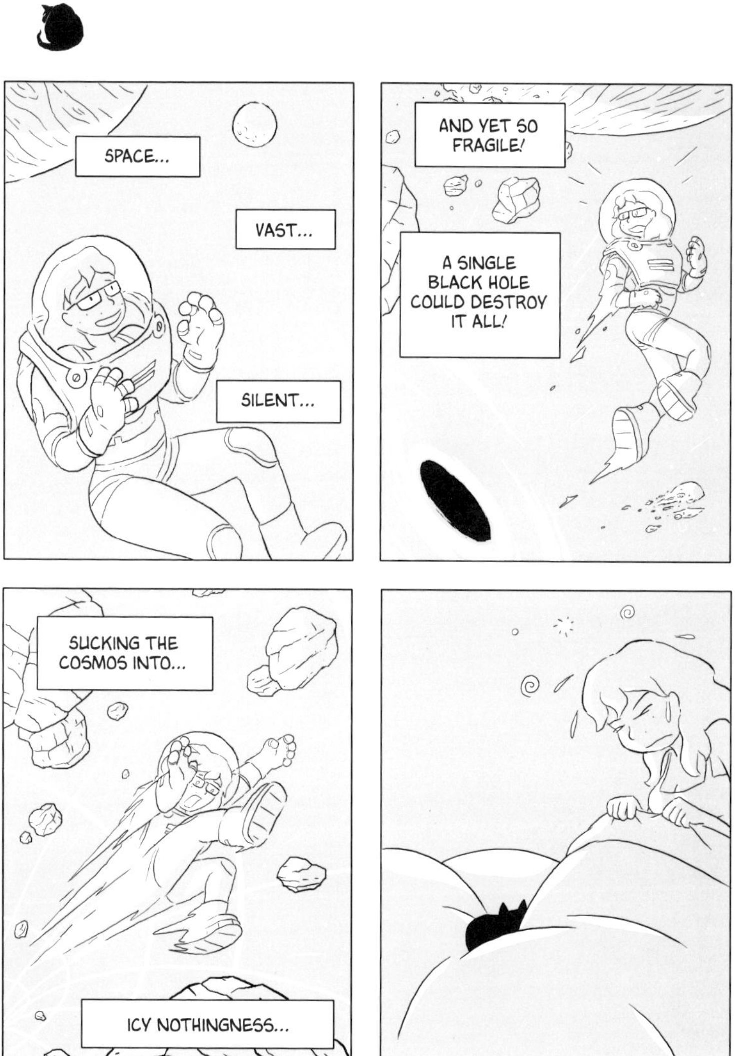
SPACE...
VAST...
SILENT...
AND YET SO FRAGILE!
A SINGLE BLACK HOLE COULD DESTROY IT ALL!
SUCKING THE COSMOS INTO...
ICY NOTHINGNESS...

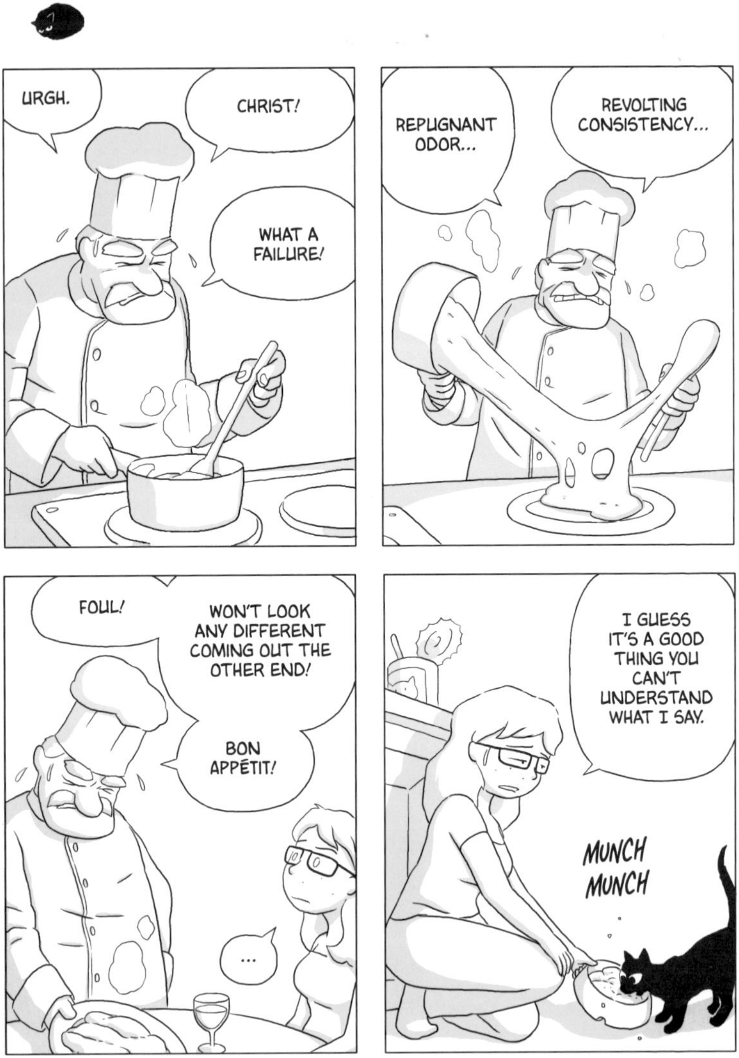
URGH.
CHRIST!
WHAT A FAILURE!
REPUGNANT ODOR...
REVOLTING CONSISTENCY...
FOUL!
WON'T LOOK ANY DIFFERENT COMING OUT THE OTHER END!
BON APPÉTIT!
...
I GUESS IT'S A GOOD THING YOU CAN'T UNDERSTAND WHAT I SAY.
MUNCH MUNCH

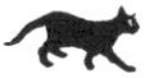

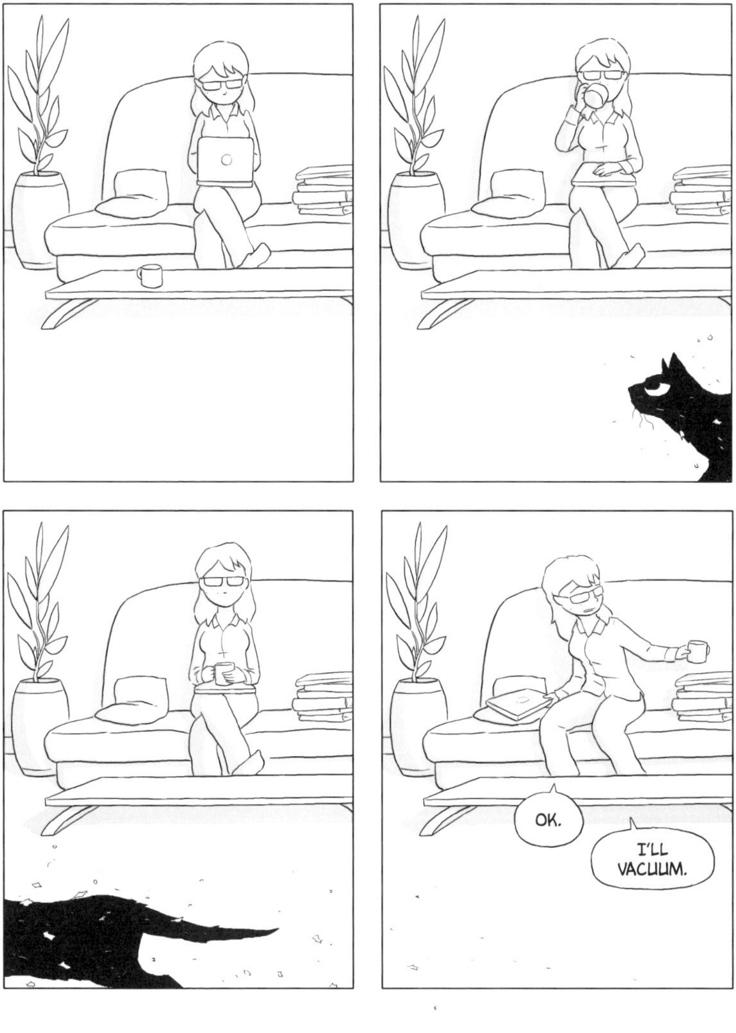
OK.
I'LL VACUUM.

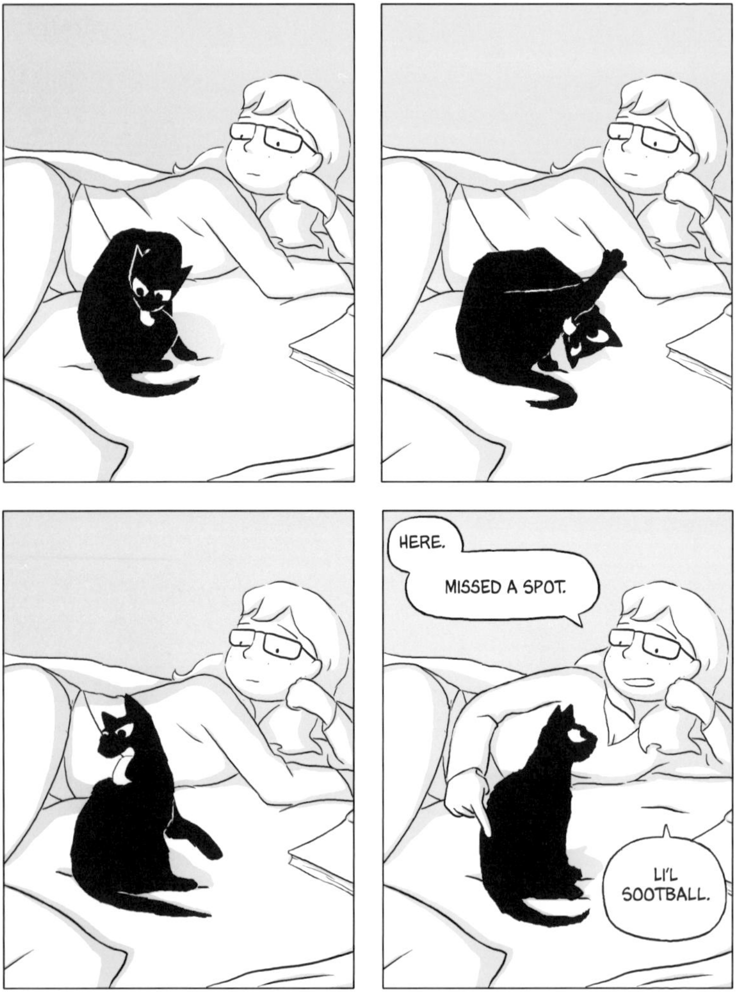
HERE.
MISSED A SPOT.
LI'L SOOTBALL.

CRITCH
CRITCH
CRITCH
CRITCH
CRI...
YOU OWE ME A BOX SPRING, SPIDER-MAN.

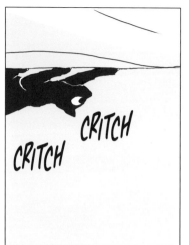

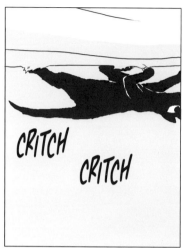

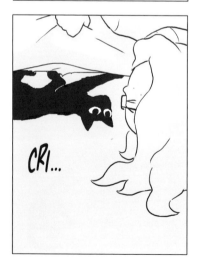

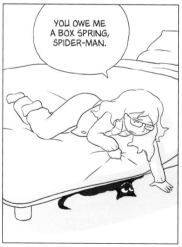

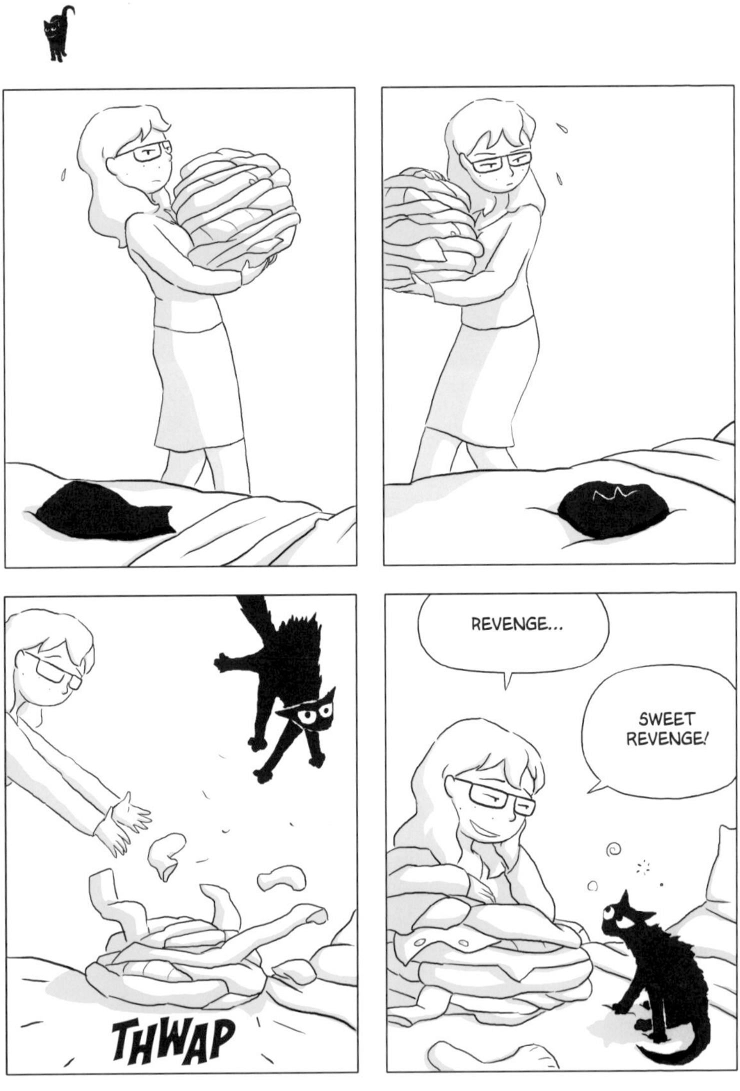
THWAP
REVENGE...
SWEET REVENGE!

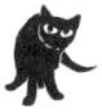
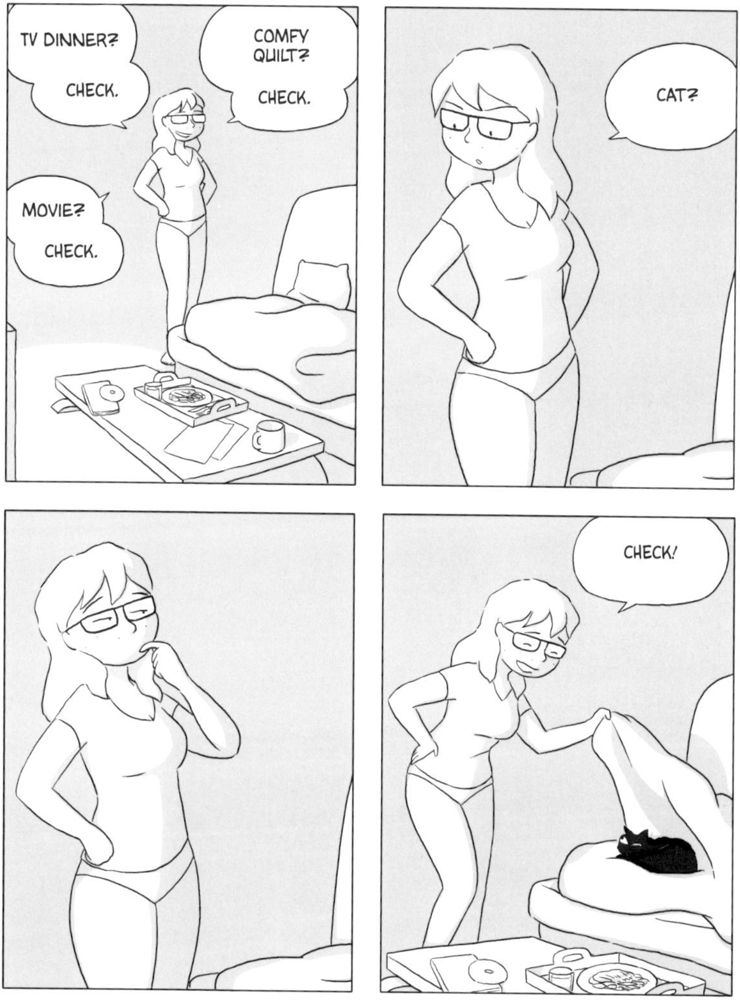
TV DINNER?
CHECK.
COMFY QUILT?
CHECK.
MOVIE?
CHECK.
CAT?
CHECK!

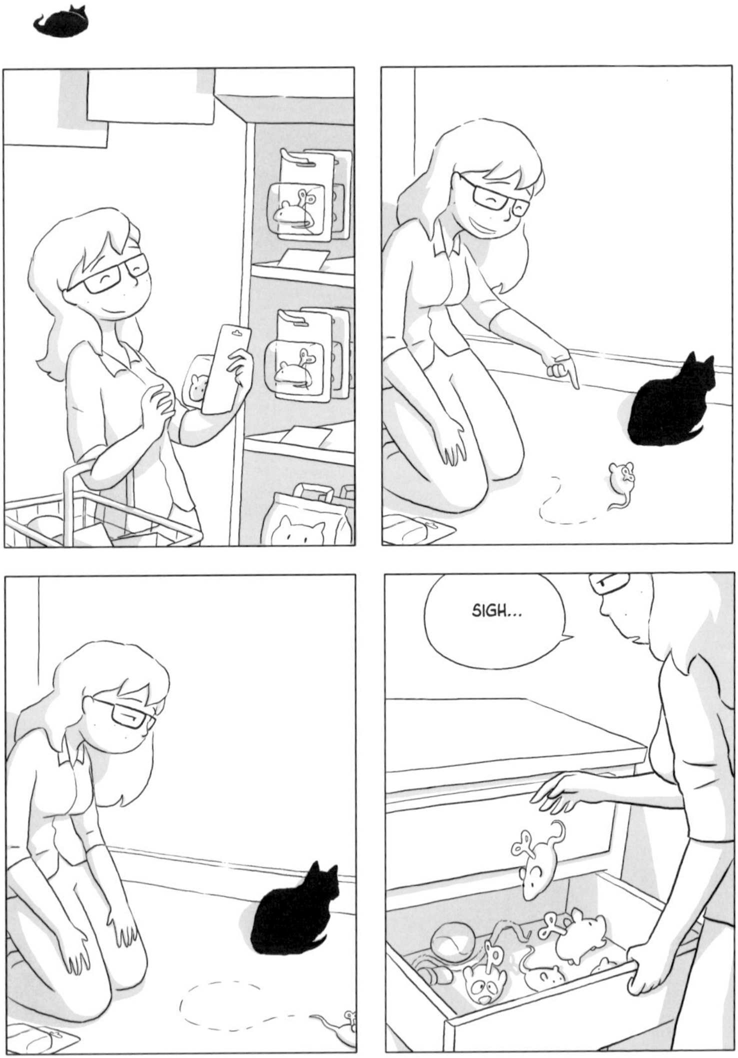
SIGH...

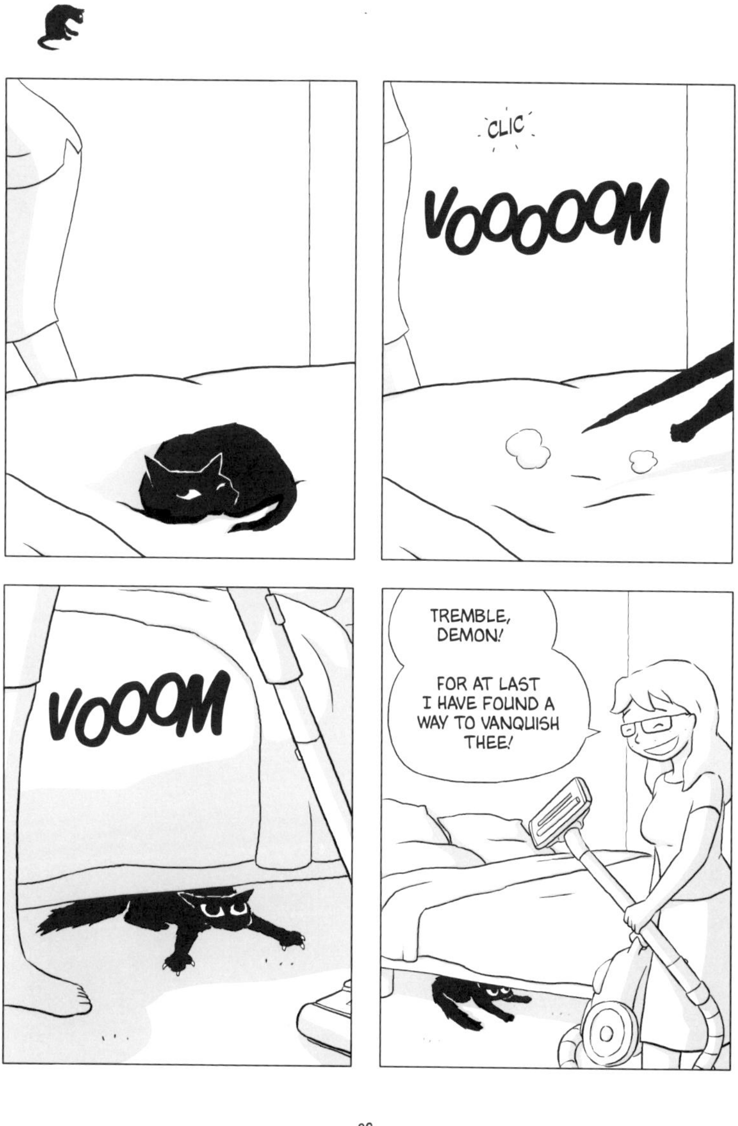
CLIC
VOOOOOM
VOOOM
TREMBLE, DEMON!
FOR AT LAST I HAVE FOUND A WAY TO VANQUISH THEE!

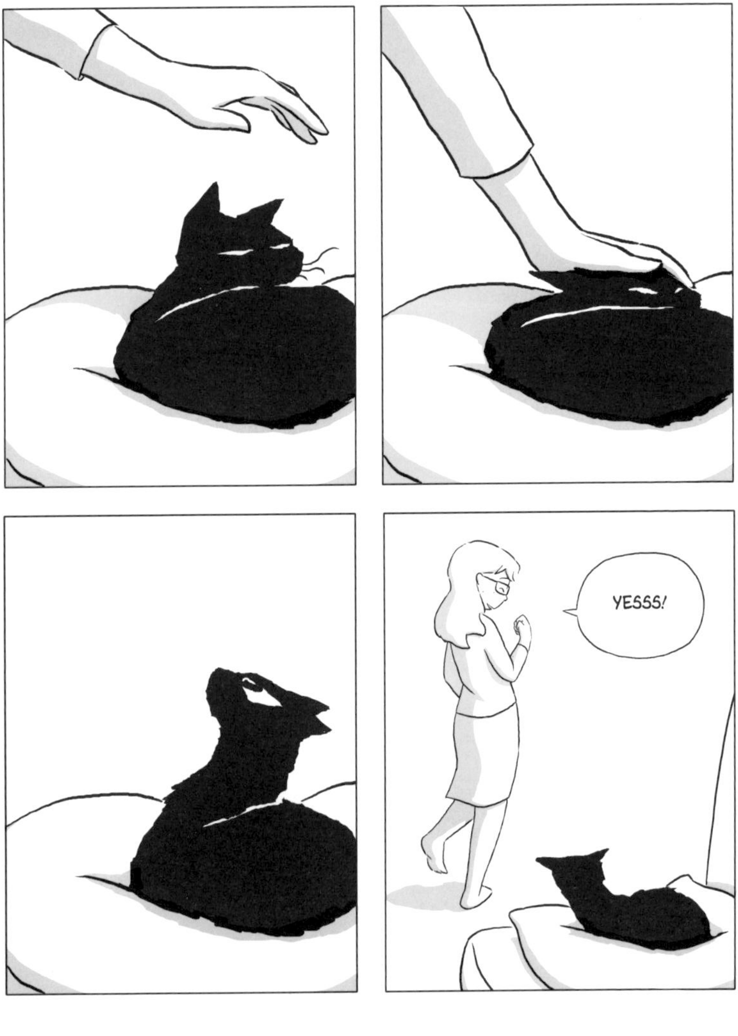
YESSS!

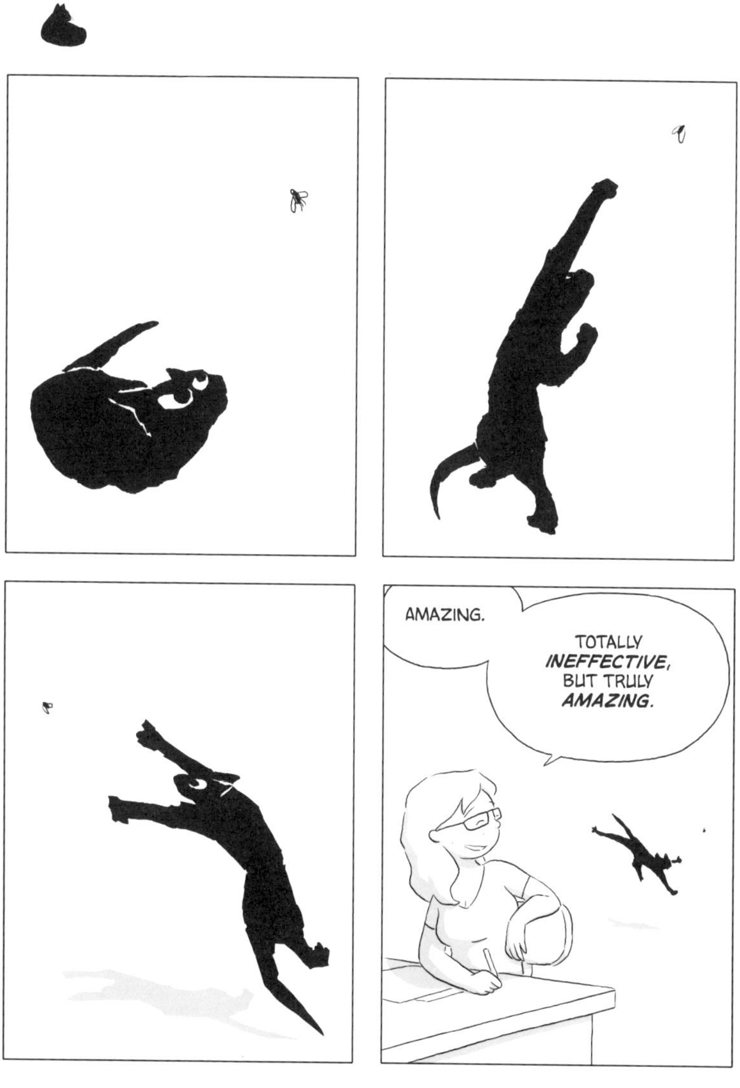
AMAZING.
TOTALLY INEFFECTIVE, BUT TRULY AMAZING.

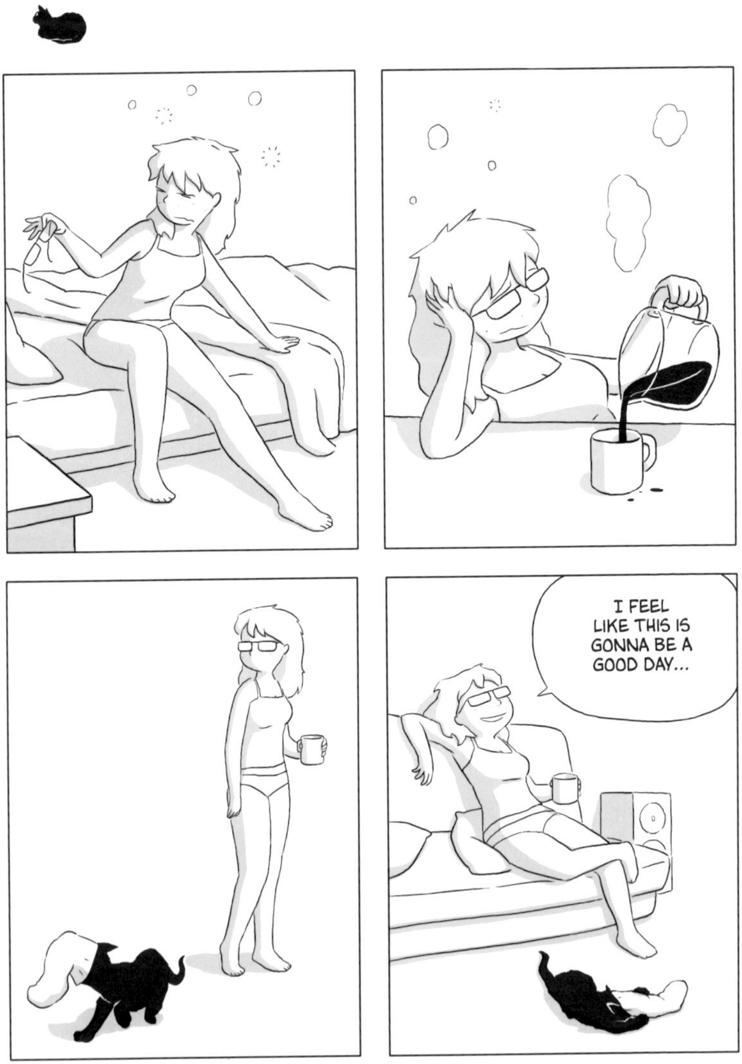
I FEEL LIKE THIS IS GONNA BE A GOOD DAY...

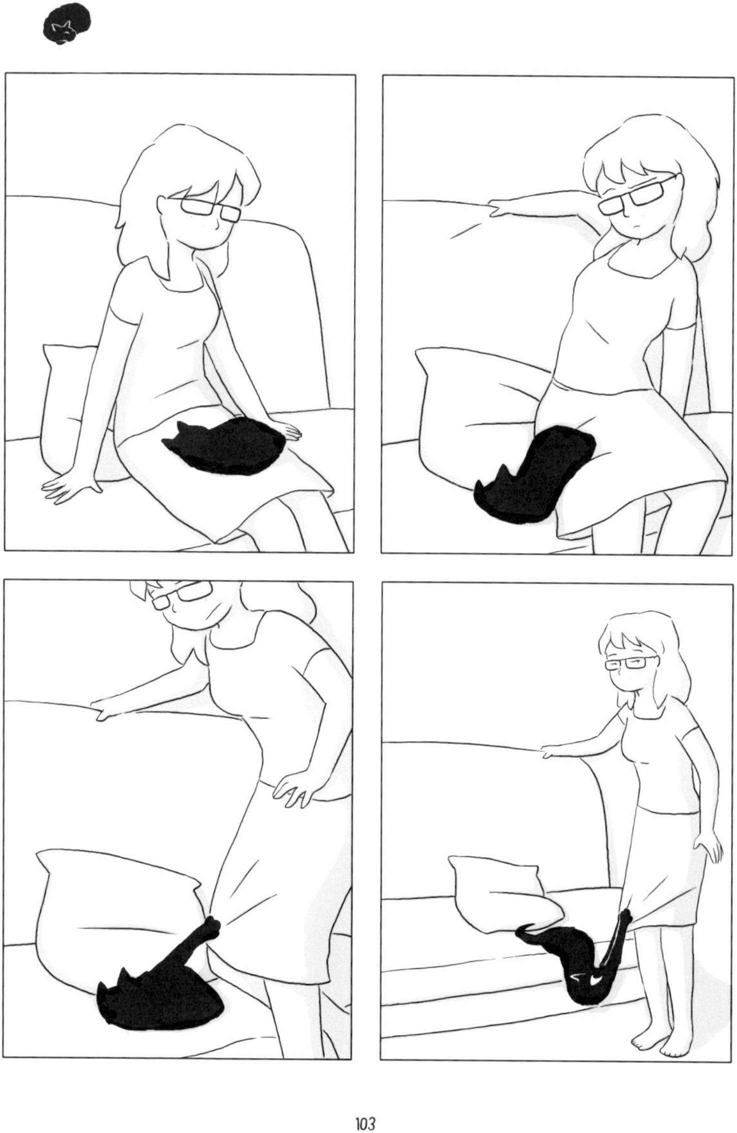

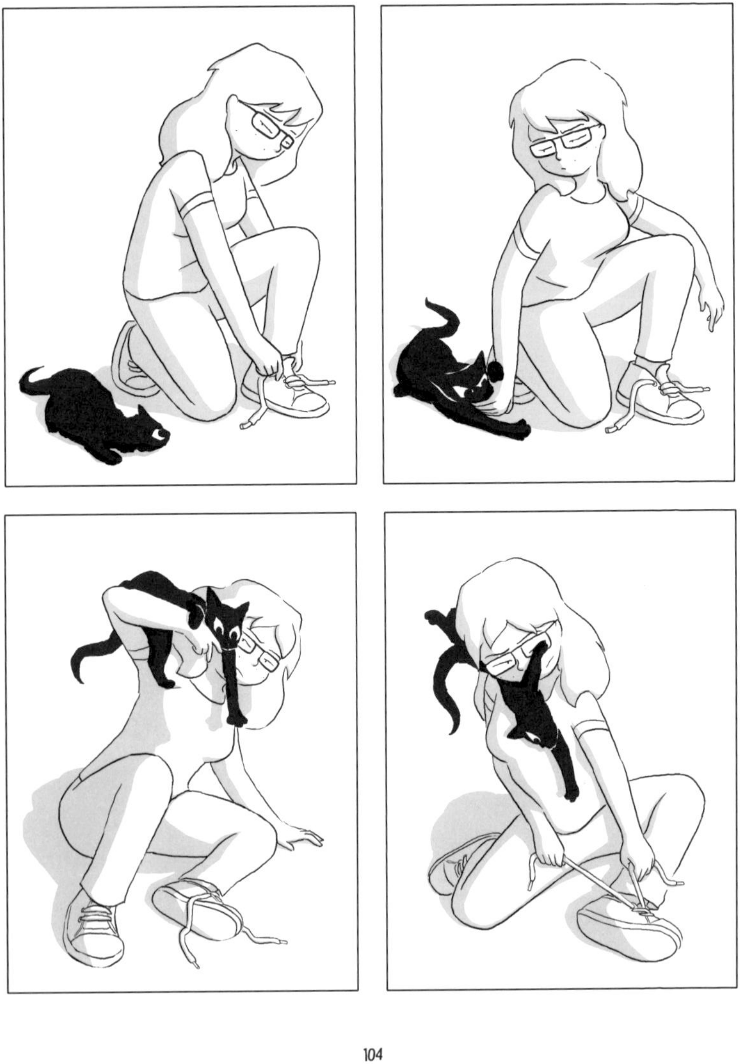

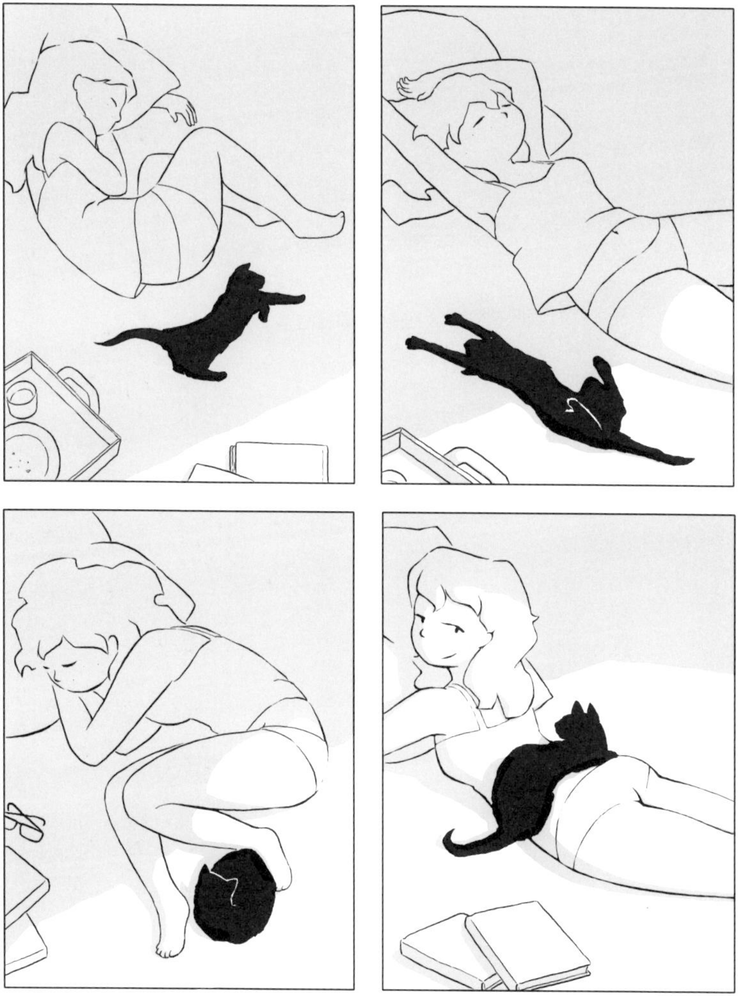

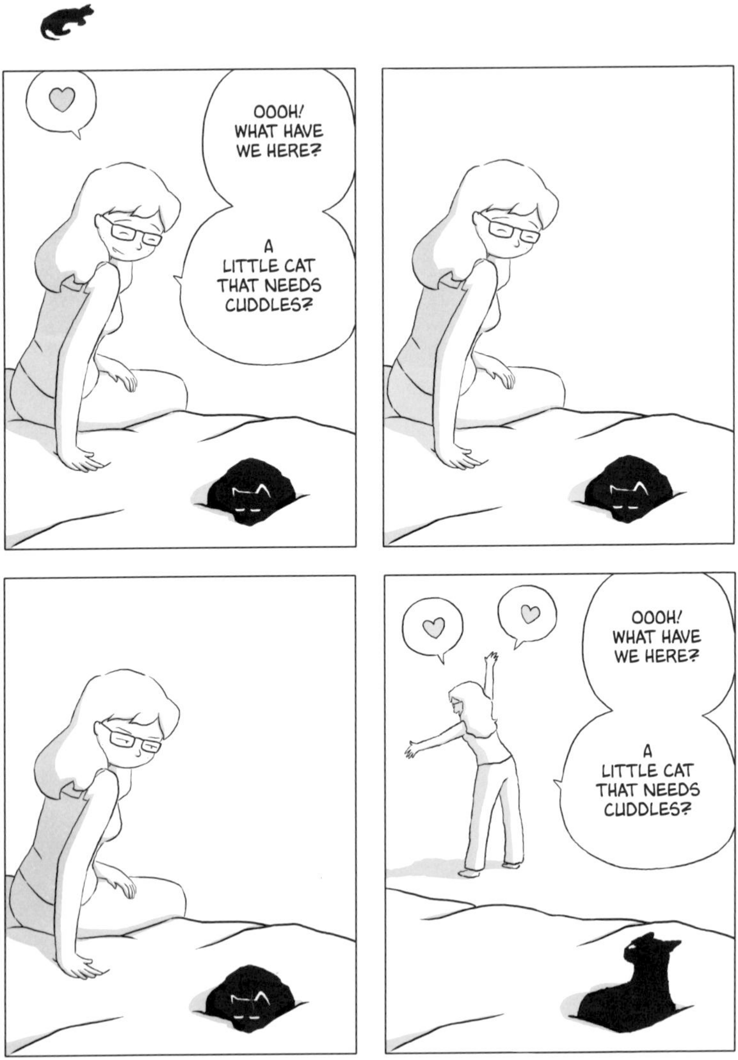
OOOH! WHAT HAVE WE HERE?
A LITTLE CAT THAT NEEDS CUDDLES?
OOOH! WHAT HAVE WE HERE?
A LITTLE CAT THAT NEEDS CUDDLES?

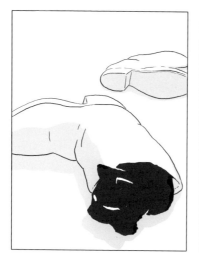

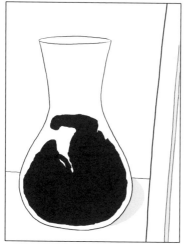

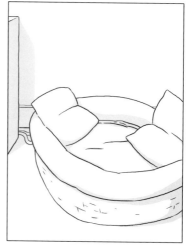

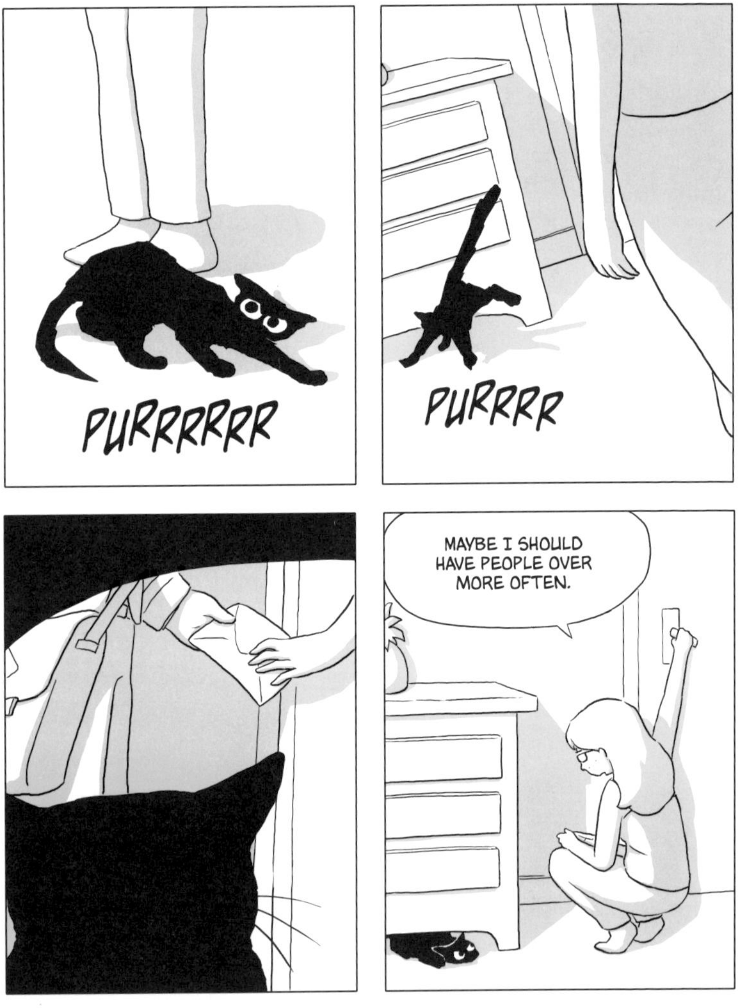
PURRRRRR
PURRRR
MAYBE I SHOULD HAVE PEOPLE OVER MORE OFTEN.

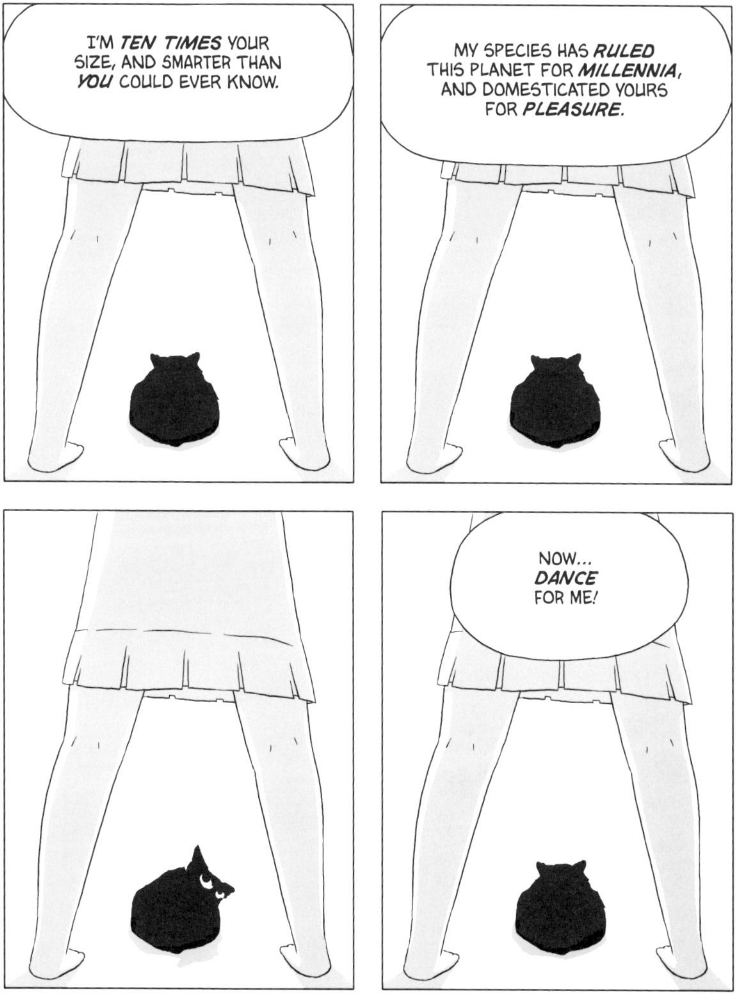
I'M TEN TIMES YOUR SIZE, AND SMARTER THAN YOU COULD EVER KNOW.
MY SPECIES HAS RULED THIS PLANET FOR MILLENNIA, AND DOMESTICATED YOURS FOR PLEASURE.
NOW... DANCE FOR ME!

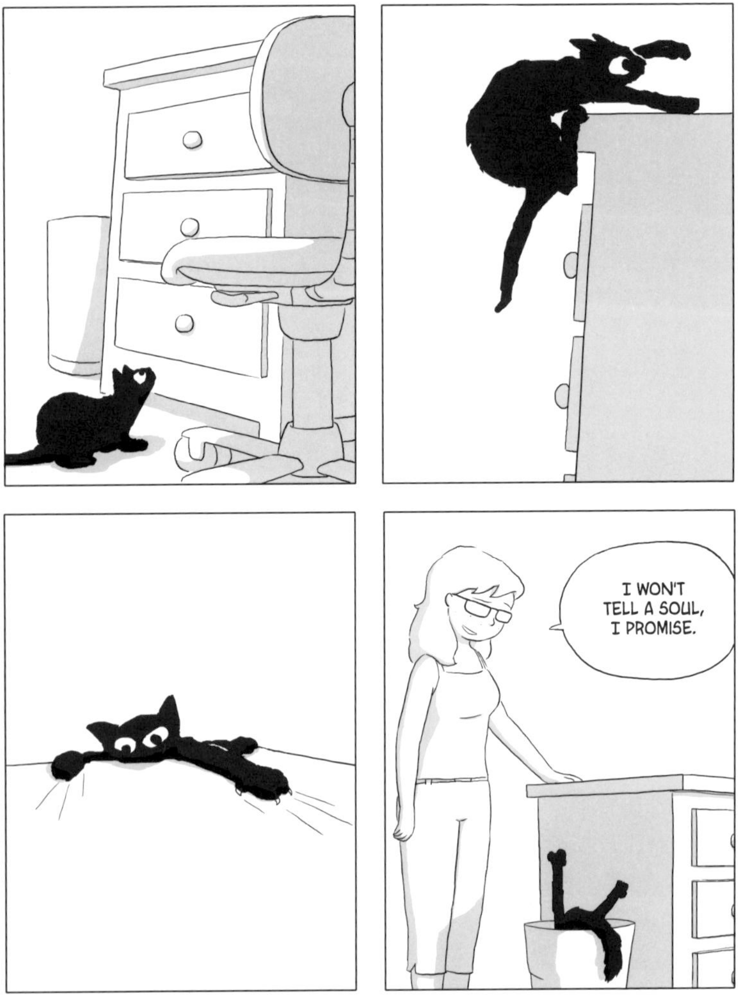
I WON'T
TELL A SOUL,
I PROMISE.

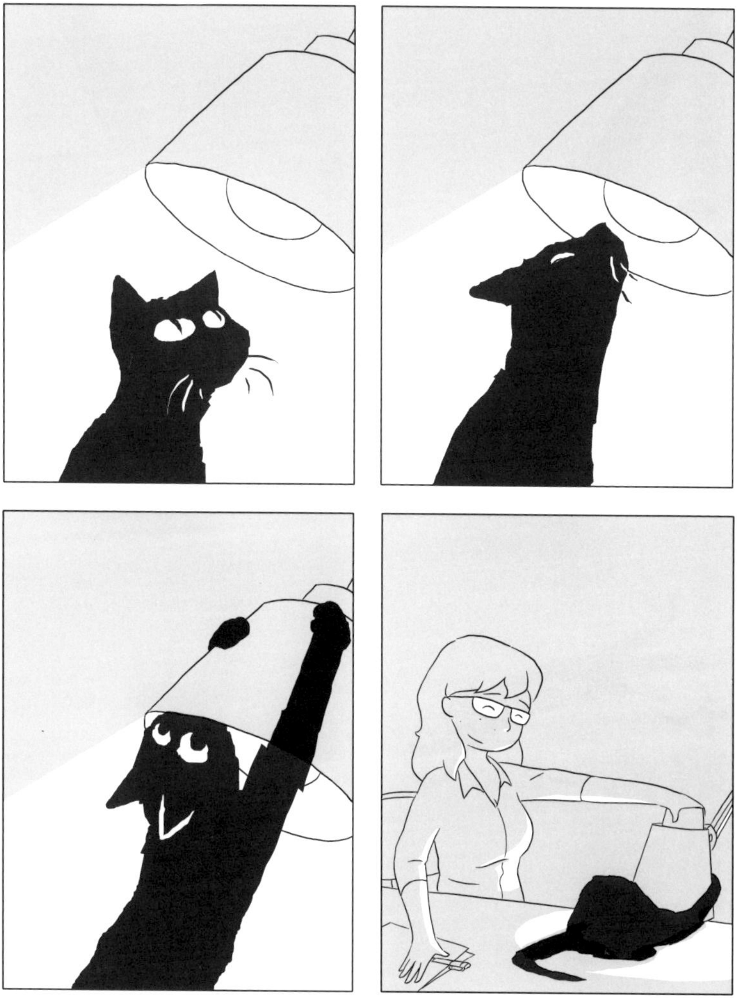

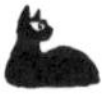
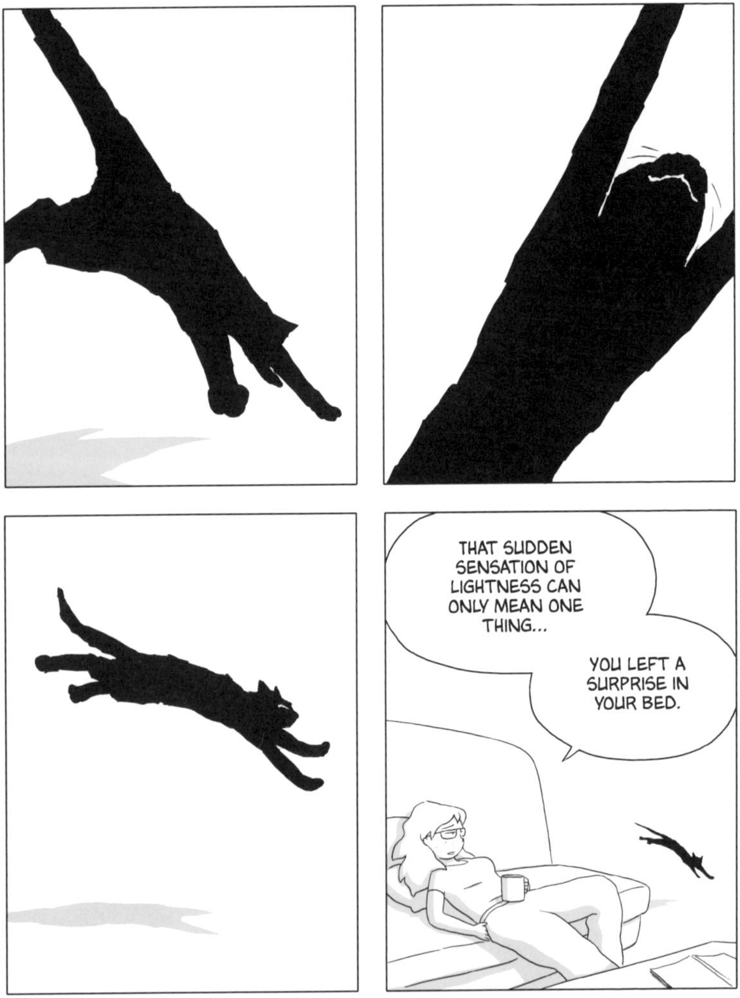
THAT SUDDEN SENSATION OF LIGHTNESS CAN ONLY MEAN ONE THING...
YOU LEFT A SURPRISE IN YOUR BED.

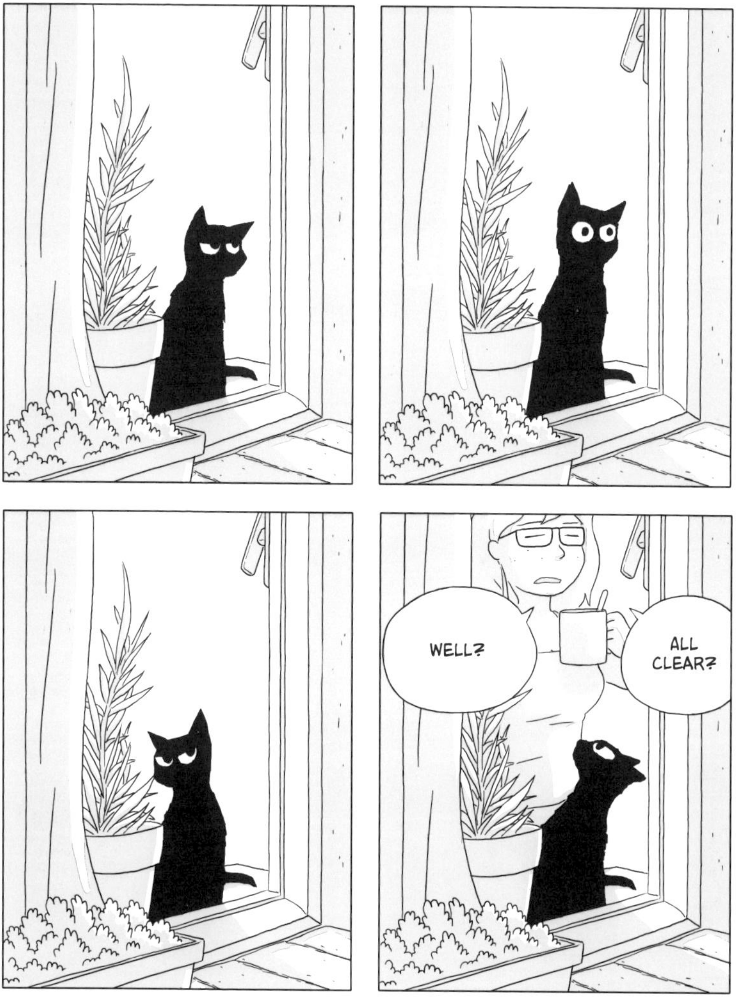
WELL?
ALL CLEAR?

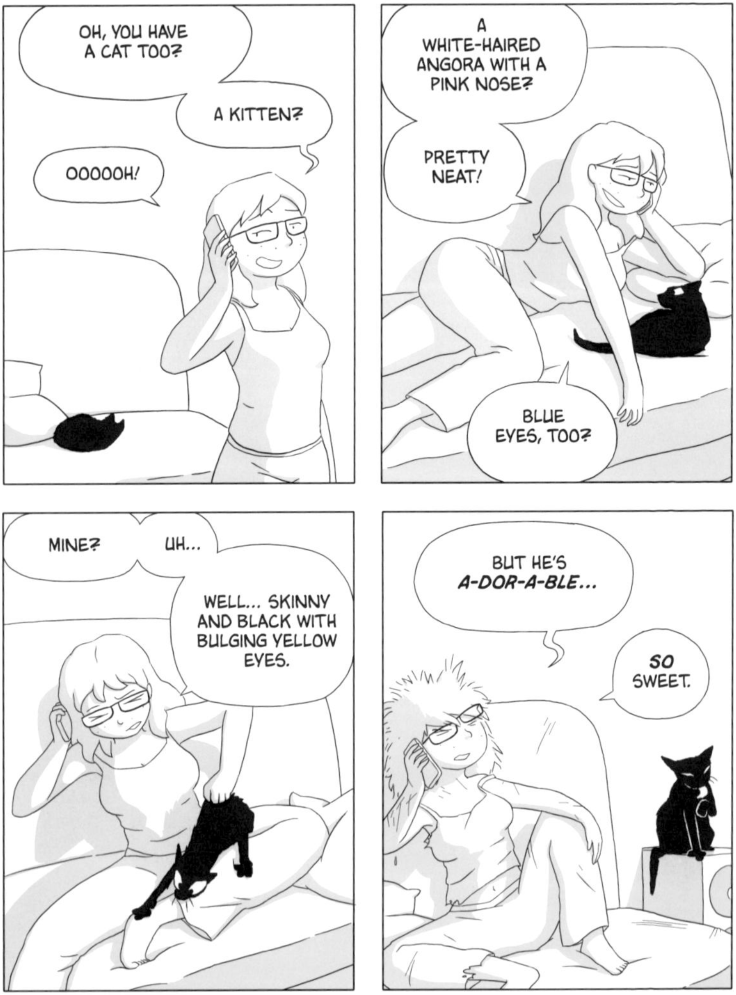
OH, YOU HAVE A CAT TOO?
A KITTEN?
OOOOOH!
A WHITE-HAIRED ANGORA WITH A PINK NOSE?
PRETTY NEAT!
BLUE EYES, TOO?
MINE?
UH...
WELL... SKINNY AND BLACK WITH BULGING YELLOW EYES.
BUT HE'S *A-DOR-A-BLE...*
SO SWEET.

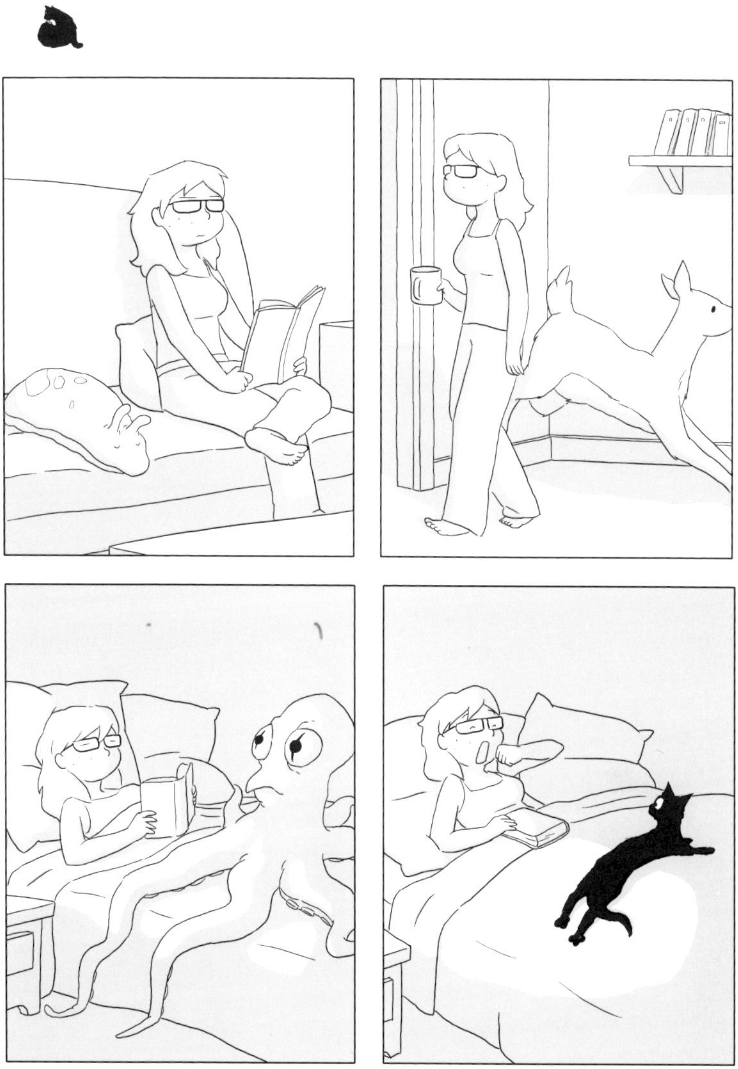

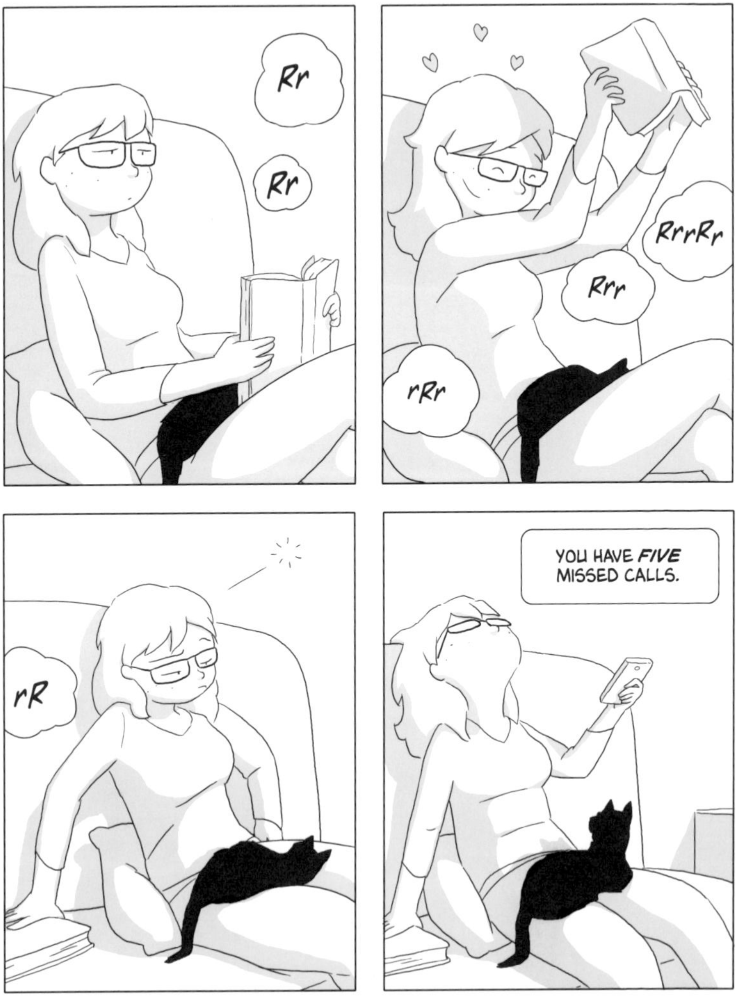
Rr
Rr
RrrRr
Rrr
rRr
rR
YOU HAVE *FIVE* MISSED CALLS.

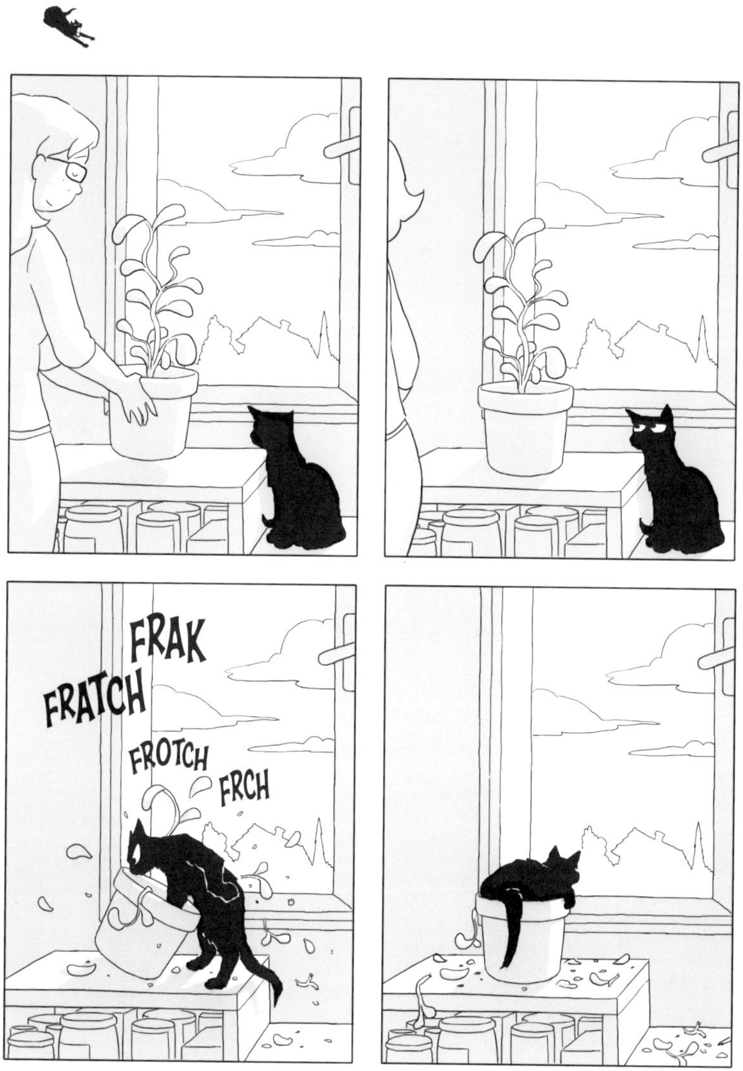
FRAK
FRATCH
FROTCH
FRCH

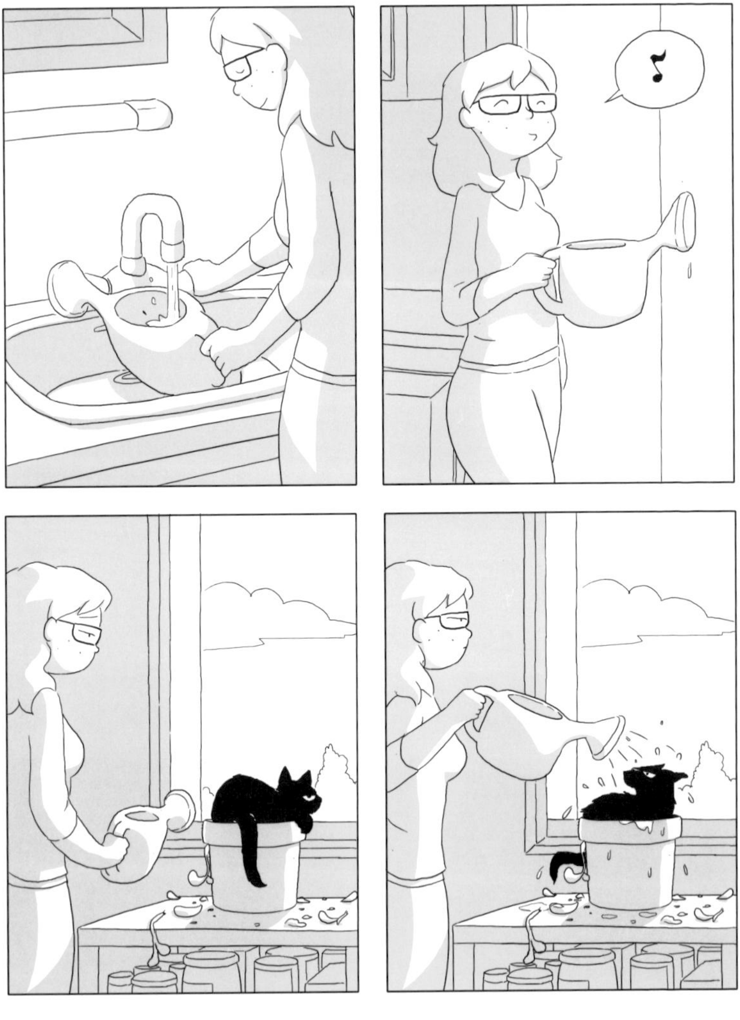

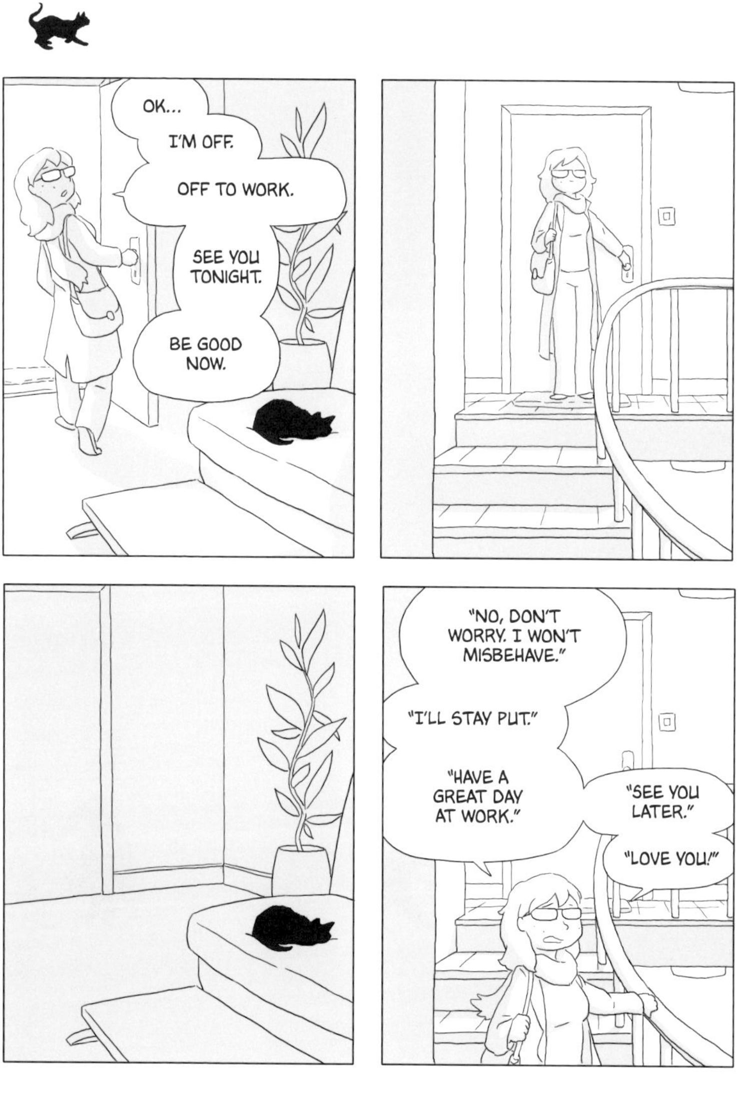
OK...
I'M OFF.
OFF TO WORK.
SEE YOU TONIGHT.
BE GOOD NOW.
"NO, DON'T WORRY. I WON'T MISBEHAVE."
"I'LL STAY PUT."
"HAVE A GREAT DAY AT WORK."
"SEE YOU LATER."
"LOVE YOU!"

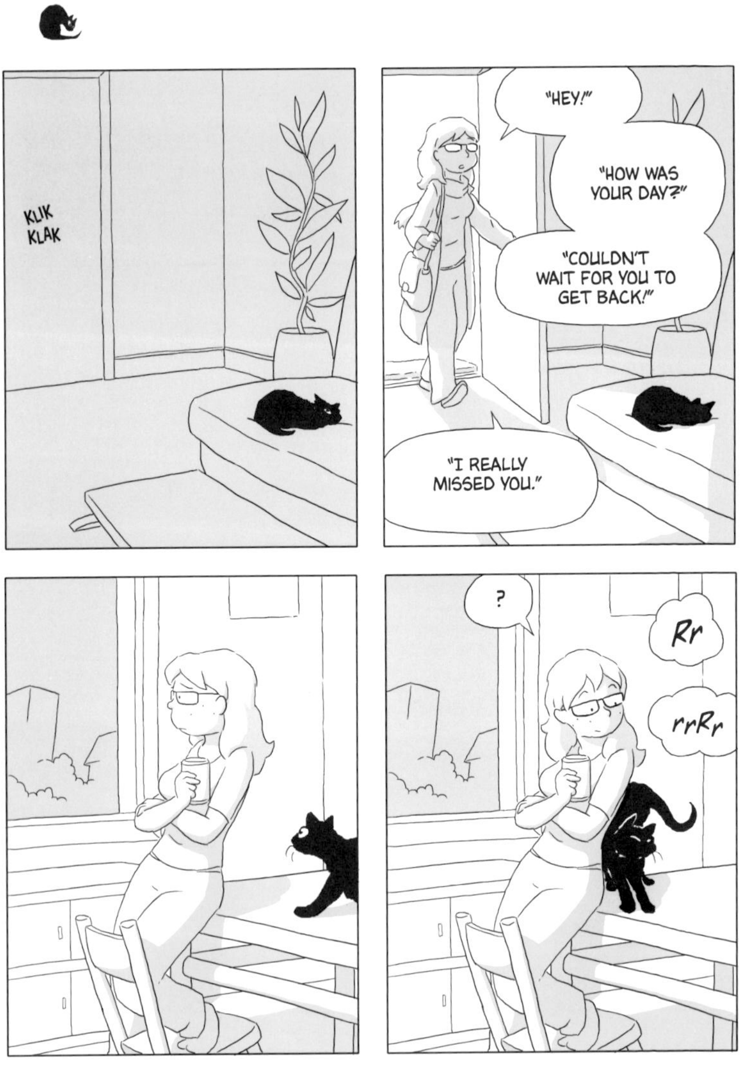
KLIK
KLAK
"HEY!"
"HOW WAS YOUR DAY?"
"COULDN'T WAIT FOR YOU TO GET BACK!"
"I REALLY MISSED YOU."
?
Rr
rrRr

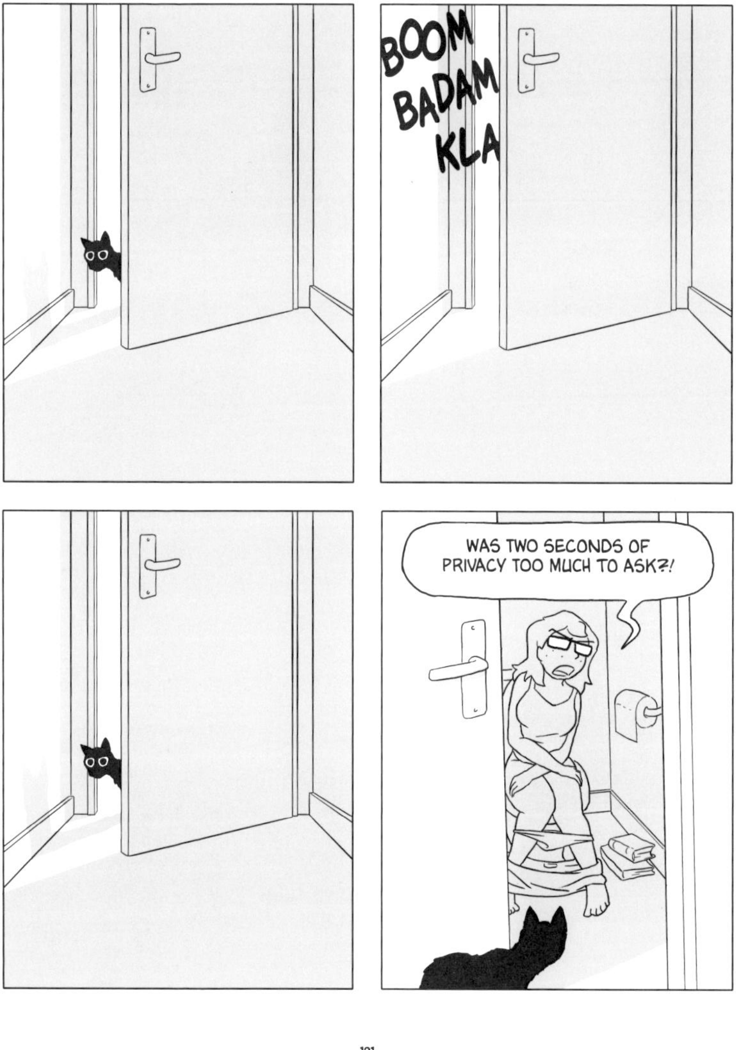
BOOM
BADAM
KLA
WAS TWO SECONDS OF PRIVACY TOO MUCH TO ASK?!

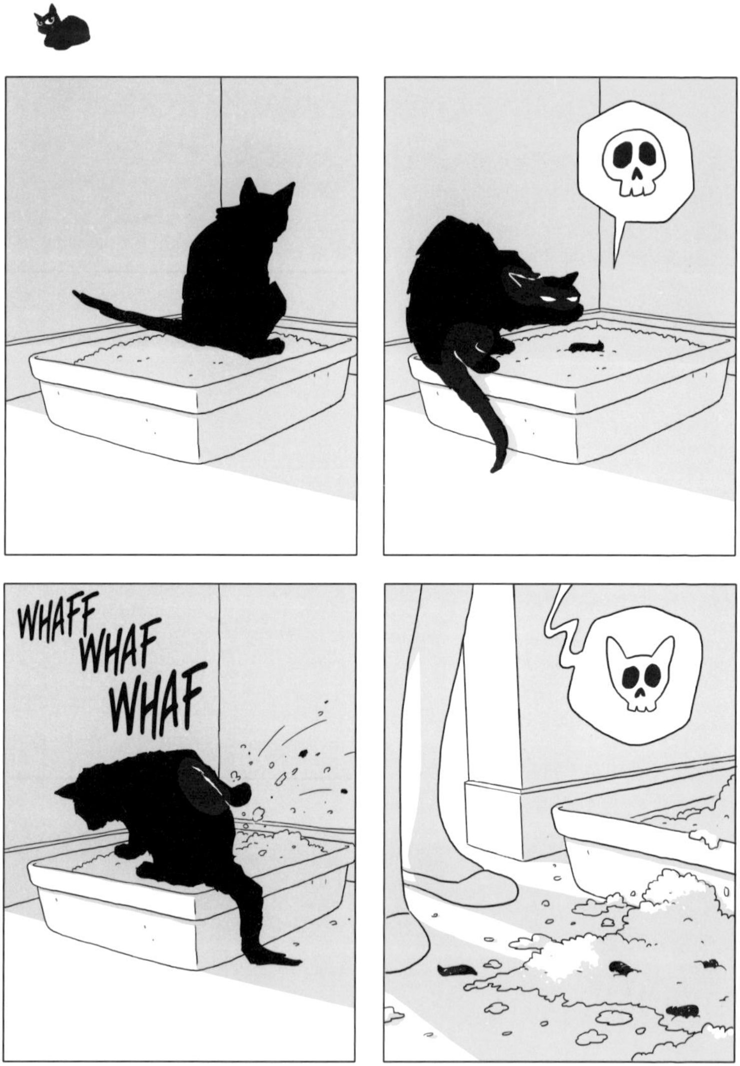
WHAFF
WHAF
WHAF

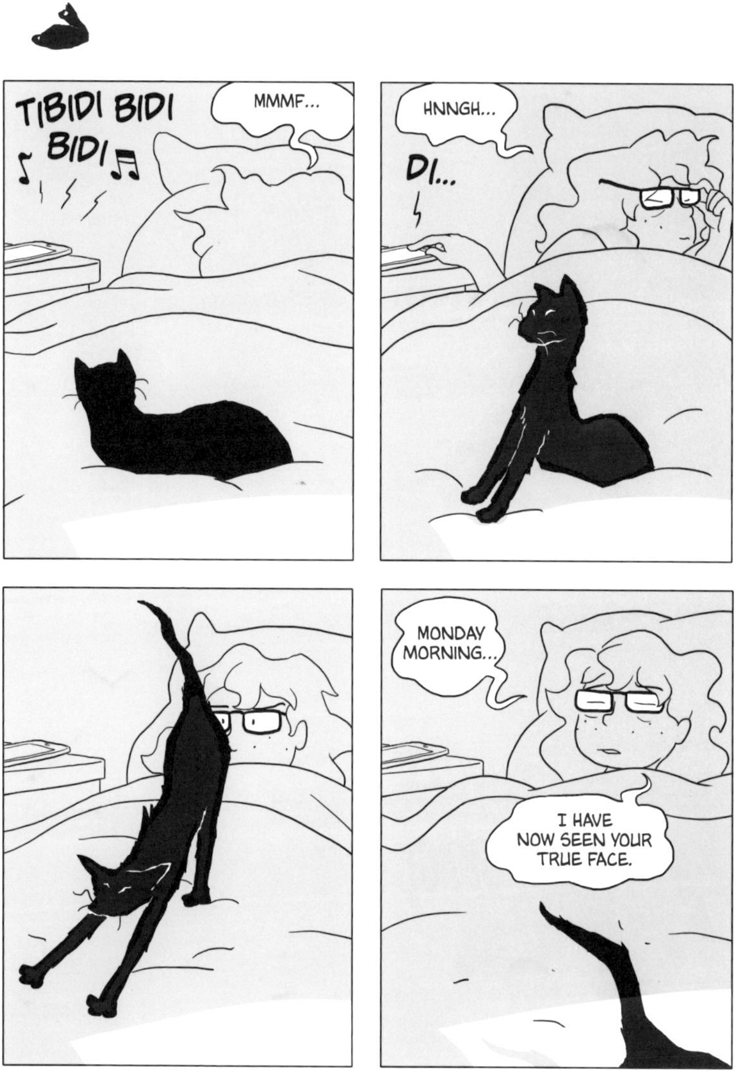
TIBIDI BIDI BIDI
MMMF...
HNNGH...
DI...
MONDAY MORNING...
I HAVE NOW SEEN YOUR TRUE FACE.

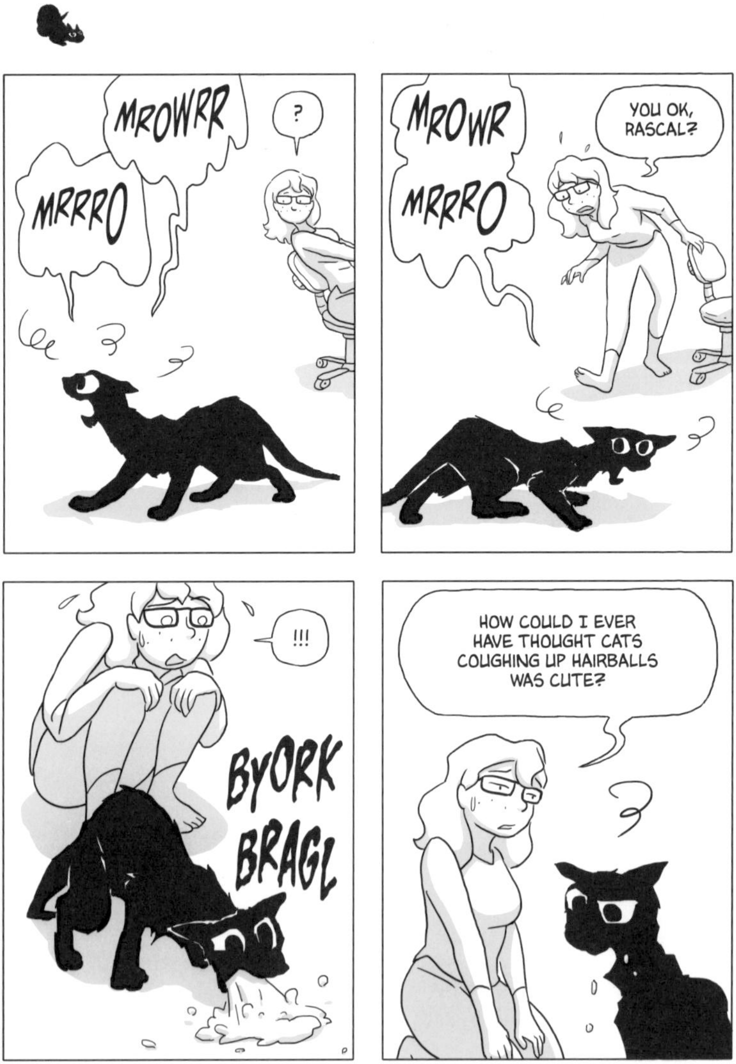
MRRRO
MROWRR
?
MROWR
MRRRO
YOU OK, RASCAL?
!!!
BYORK
BRAGL
HOW COULD I EVER HAVE THOUGHT CATS COUGHING UP HAIRBALLS WAS CUTE?

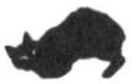

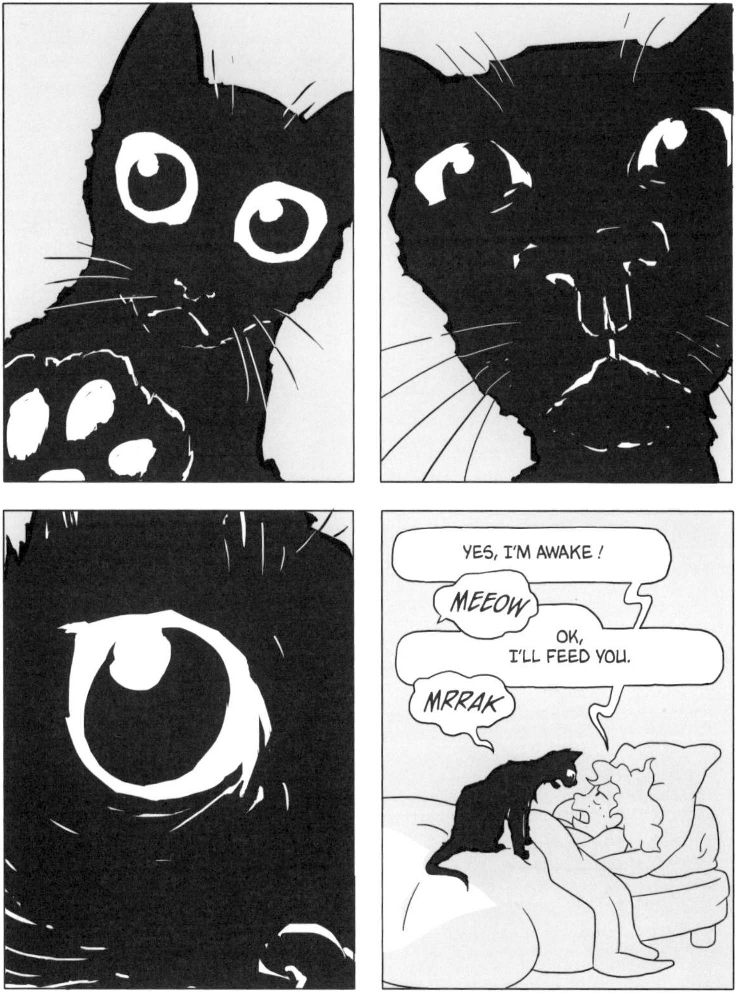
YES, I'M AWAKE !
MEEOW
OK, I'LL FEED YOU.
MRRAK

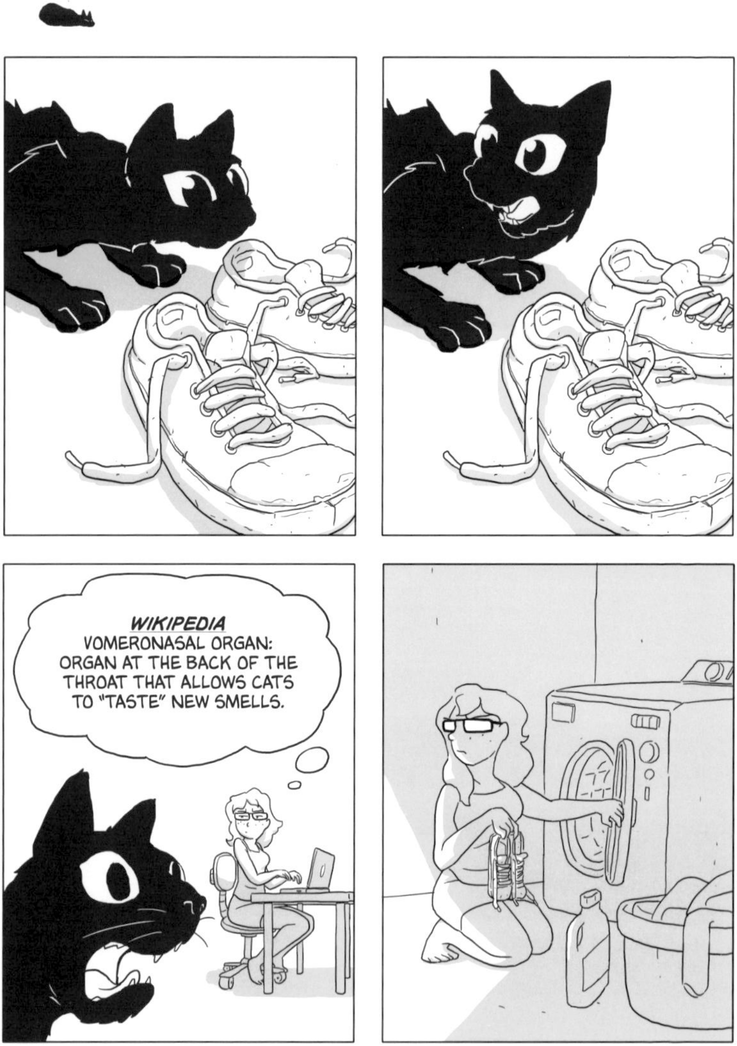
WIKIPEDIA
VOMERONASAL ORGAN: ORGAN AT THE BACK OF THE THROAT THAT ALLOWS CATS TO "TASTE" NEW SMELLS.

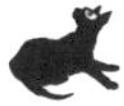

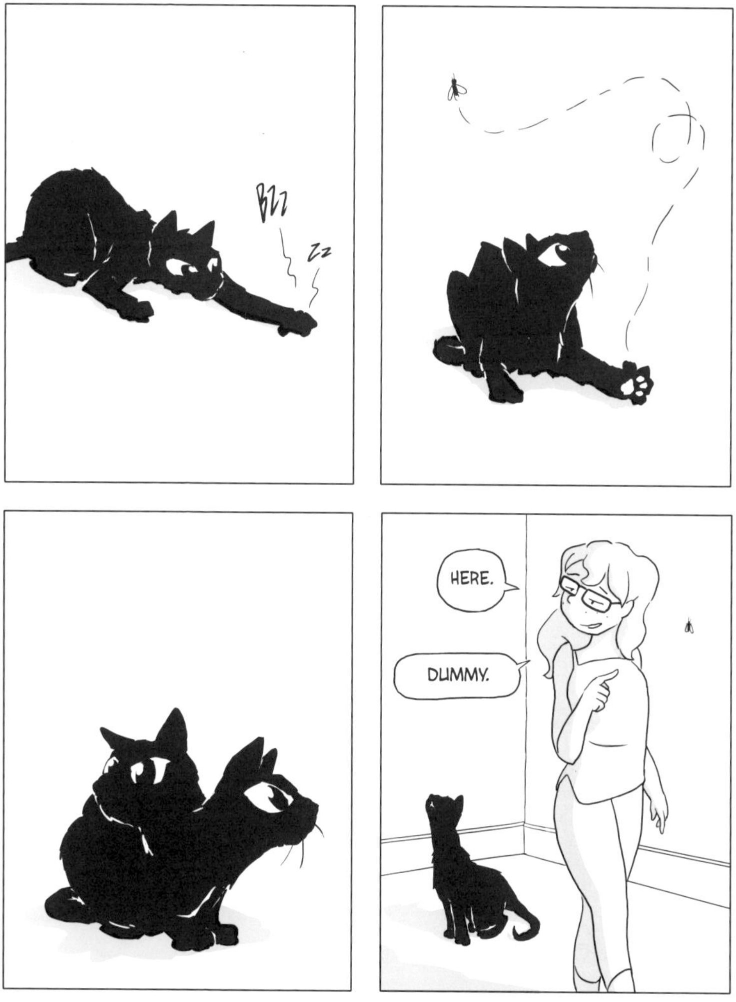
BZZ
ZZ
HERE.
DUMMY.

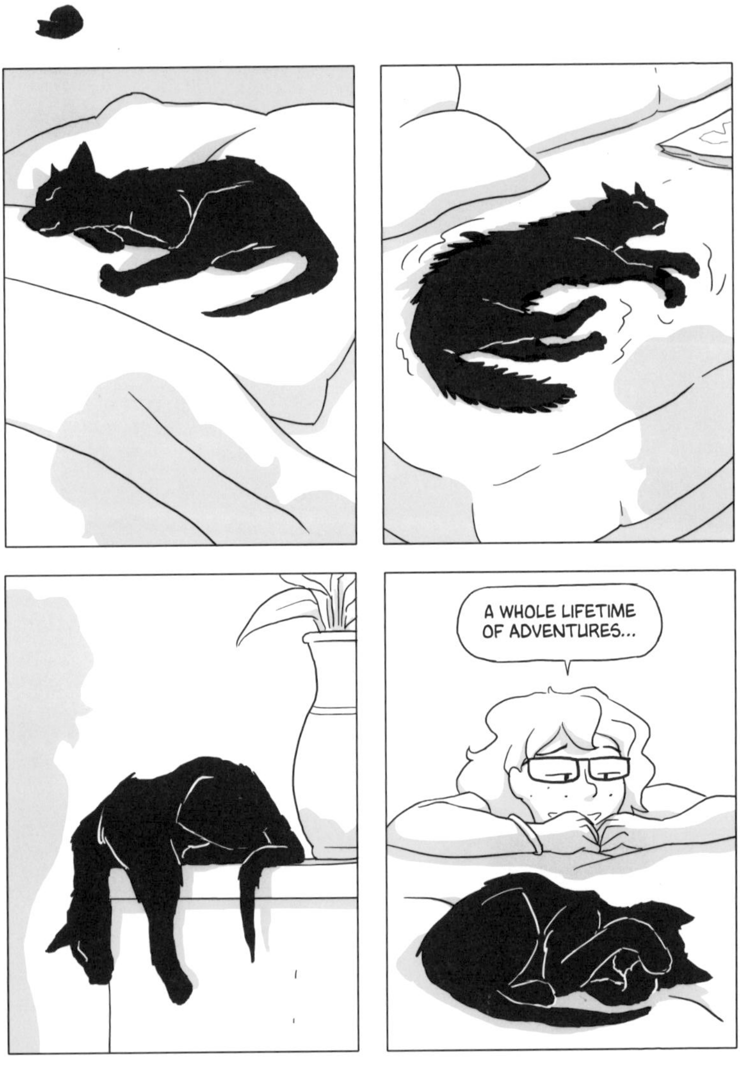
A WHOLE LIFETIME OF ADVENTURES...

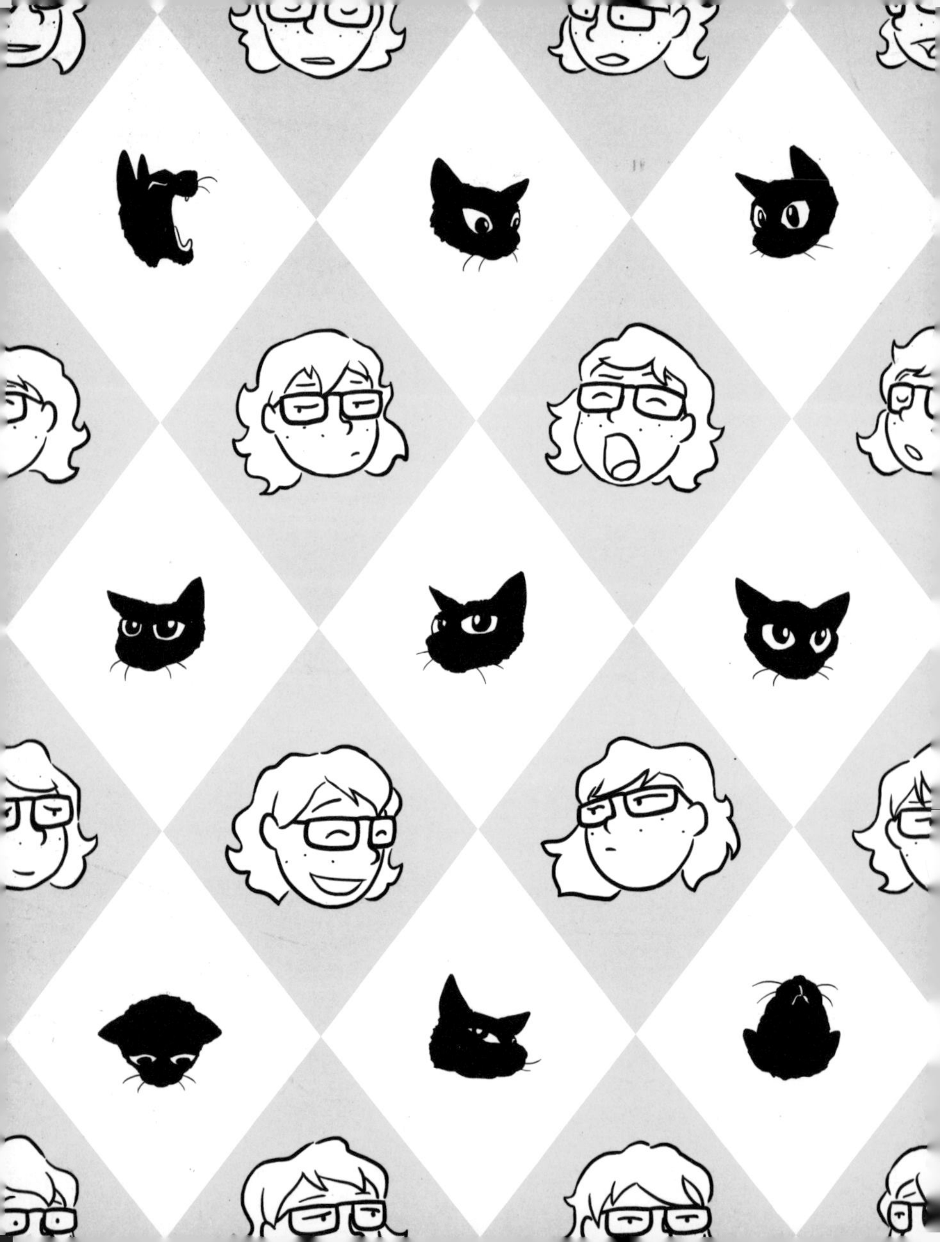